CONTENTS

FOREWORD

It is important, when considering the subject of First Aid for the first time, that the reader should obtain a clear picture of those facts and procedures which constitute the elements of First Aid.

With this basic knowledge he or she becomes immediately a person of greater value to the community and is in a position to improve his skill, to study if desired more advanced techniques, and to increase his knowledge of anatomy and physiology in their relationship to First Aid.

In this book Dr. A. S. Playfair has set out to give a simple presentation of the essentials of First Aid. Lengthy descriptions have been avoided so far as possible and visual methods of presentation are widely used, with the result that the book makes easy and interesting reading.

The British Red Cross Society is grateful to Dr. Playfair for having written this valuable Manual.

Although primarily produced for young people, the Manual should be regarded by those of all ages as a presentation of basic First Aid, a subject which may subsequently be studied with advantage in greater detail.

Medical Adviser, British Red Cross Society.

SCOPE OF FIRST AID

what is first aid?

Note that it is called FIRST-aid.
It is the help given at once to injured people or to those taken suddenly ill before the expert (doctor or nurse) takes over or the ambulance arrives.

the object of first aid is:

To save life.
To prevent the injury becoming worse.
To help recovery.

the good first aider's task is:

To find out what has happened.
To deal with the condition or the illness.
To reassure and protect the person from further danger.
To arrange for him to be taken home or to hospital.

what equipment is needed?

Really none. Though first-aid kits contain many useful things (such as bandages and dressings) the GOOD first-aider does not depend on them. He uses ordinary, everyday articles available at hand, and improvises when no first-aid equipment is available.

how we breathe

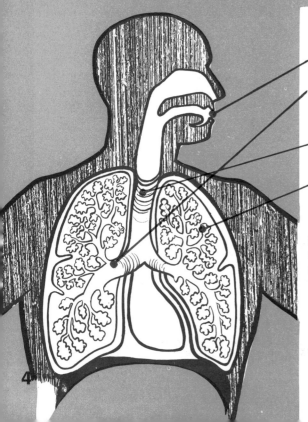

By using muscles to expand our chests we draw air into the lungs.
From the **nose** and **mouth** the air passes down the **windpipe** (which goes down the neck) into the chest and then branches into a right and a left **main air tube**, one for each of the two lungs.
Each tube now divides very many times into smaller ones. The last tiny divisions end in microscopic **air sacs.** The collection of air sacs (which are far smaller and much more numerous than can be shown in the diagram), forms the bulk of the lungs.
To breathe out, the chest contracts, compressing the lungs, so sending some of the gas contents back up through the windpipe into the air.

Usually we breathe in and out about sixteen times a minute. This may be faster in babies and small children and in some illnesses. We can count the breathing rate by watching movements of the chest or of the clothes covering it.

why we breathe

All parts of the body use OXYGEN for life and energy. In so doing they produce another gas, CARBON DIOXIDE. This carbon dioxide is waste matter and is removed, dissolved in the blood.

Air contains oxygen.

Each time we breathe in we take fresh oxygen into our lungs.

From the air sacs of the lungs, the oxygen passes into a surrounding network of small blood vessels known as capillaries (see page 17).

Dissolved in the blood, the oxygen is carried by other vessels to reach all parts of the body.

At the same time the carbon dioxide, brought to the lungs by the blood, passes from the network into the air sacs to be breathed out of the body.

SUFFOCATION (ASPHYXIA) occurs when air cannot pass in and out of the lungs.

We must breathe to live.

Without oxygen we would die.

If we could not get rid of unwanted carbon dioxide we would die.

Smothering or choking may mean death.

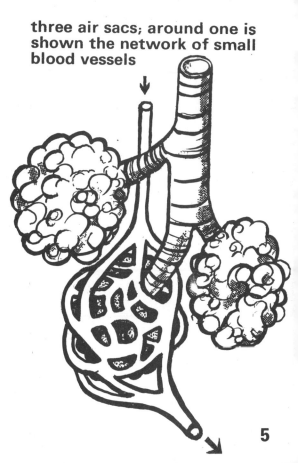

three air sacs; around one is shown the network of small blood vessels

5

SMOTHERING

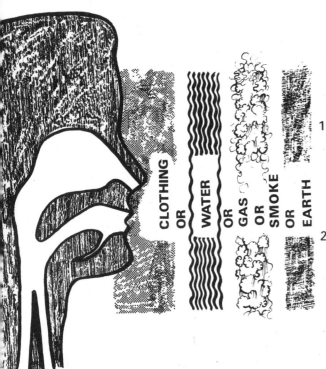

CLOTHING OR | WATER OR | GAS OR SMOKE OR EARTH

Smothering means that air cannot even get into the mouth or nose. **Clothing** or a **plastic bag** over the head can smother. So can **drowning** (water instead of air), **gassing** (smoke or fumes instead of air), or a **fall of earth** burying the patient.

1. Immediately remove the obstruction from the head, or take the patient from the water or from the fume-laden atmosphere. (In gas or fumes be careful to breathe as little as you can of the contaminated air yourself; act quickly and hold your breath as long as you can).
A person buried under earth or sand will need to have this material cleared away down to his waist as well, so that the chest can expand to allow breathing.

2. **Without further delay** give artificial respiration (see page 8).

CHOKING

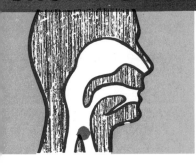

Choking happens when the windpipe is blocked.

This could arise from food or vomit 'going down the wrong way' or if a small object, held in the mouth, suddenly slips back.

In STRANGLING the windpipe is blocked by a tight band round the neck.

A choking patient may be coughing; he will be struggling for breath and blue in the face.

what to do

1. Give several hard thumps between the shoulder blades to try to loosen the matter in the windpipe. Try to hook out with a finger anything blocking the back of the throat. A small child can be held, firmly, upside down.

   In STRANGLING quickly loosen or cut the tight band but support the patient to prevent his falling.

2. If, when the obstruction is freed, the patient is not breathing give artificial respiration at once (see page 8).

WORK FAST DO NOT DELAY.

When the patient has stopped breathing for himself the rescuer tries to revive him by getting air into his lungs by other means.

If artificial respiration is needed the matter is urgent.

It cannot be stressed enough that in this emergency NO TIME CAN BE WASTED. Resuscitation must begin AT ONCE with no moments spared to place the patient's (or rescuer's) body comfortably. A drowned person, for instance, must receive artificial respiration as soon as his head is free from the water.

DELAY OF ONE OR TWO SECONDS MAY PROVE FATAL.

At the most, if the first-aider suspects that the patient's throat is badly blocked-by false teeth, mud or weeds for instance-he may try to clear this by one quick, thorough scoop of his finger, sweeping the back of the mouth.

Once artificial respiration has been given for two or three minutes with air coming freely in and out of the lungs then, and only then, may attention be paid to other details of positioning the patient, of covering him, seeking additional help and so on. But all the time the rescuer must continue to give artificial respiration and keep careful watch.

Two methods are taught.

1. **Mouth-to-mouth (or mouth-to-nose).** The rescuer breathes air from his own lungs into the patient's lungs, through the patient's mouth or nose. Even though this is air breathed out by the rescuer it still holds enough oxygen for the purpose.

2. **Holger Nielsen** is the alternative used when injuries to the patient's face make the first method impossible. The rescuer by manipulating the patient's arms and chest alternately, expands and compresses the lungs and so moves air in and out of them.

positioning the head

Though it has been stressed that no time should be wasted moving the patient's body to special positions before giving artificial respiration, one thing is essential: THE HEAD MUST BE HELD TILTED WELL BACK WITH THE LOWER JAW PUSHED FORWARD.

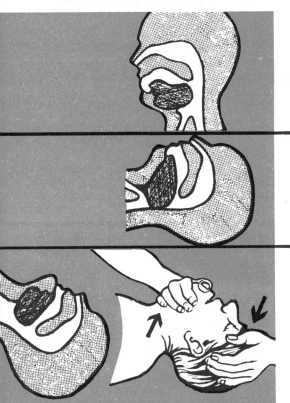

When a healthy conscious person is breathing there is plenty of space for the air to move from the mouth and nose to the windpipe.

With an unconscious patient lying on his back the tongue is likely to fall backwards, blocking the space between the mouth and the windpipe. Air cannot get through.

However if now:
1. The patient's head is pressed back, so that the nostrils look direct upwards.
2. His lower jaw is pushed forward so that the chin juts out then the tongue moves forward with the lower jaw and the air passages are opened.

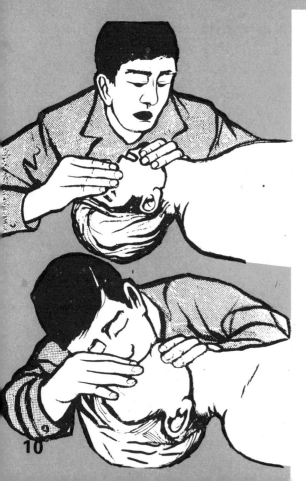

(Make sure you have read pages 8 and 9).

1. Pinch the nostrils shut with the fingers of one hand and keep the head right back.
2. With the fingers and the thumb of the other hand press the lower jaw forward so that the chin juts out. At the same time get the mouth open. **Maintain in this position all the time.**
3. Take a deep breath.
4. Open your mouth wide. Seal your lips round the patient's open mouth.
5. Blow firmly, but gently, into the patient's mouth and so into his lungs.
6. Lift your mouth off, turning your head to look at the patient's chest. If you have been successful you will see that it has risen and is now falling as the air comes out.

The above may seem an intricate series of steps. It is not. With practice it can be done as one move which immediately gives air to the patient.

7. Repeat 3, 4, 5 and 6 for four full, quick breaths. This will load the patient's blood with oxygen. His colour should improve.
8. Now continue at a steady deliberate rate, watching the rise of the chest as guarantee that air is entering the lungs and blowing in again as soon as the chest has fallen.

If the chest does not rise, check for obstruction in the throat (see treatment of choking, page 7).

For the method used on a child, see page 14

important safeguards in the mouth to mouth method

(The numbers below correspond to the instructions on the opposite page)

1. Pinch the nostrils (not the bony bridge or the extreme tip of the nose).
2. (a) Get the head back far enough. You should be able to look vertically down on the now closed nostrils.
   (b) Keep your fingers away from the patient's lips so that your own lips can form a perfect seal.
4. Open your mouth widely enough so that it makes a complete seal round the patient's mouth.
5. (a) Blow from your chest, and not from your cheeks.
   (b) Blow only hard enough to make the patient's chest rise.
6. If the chest has not moved, check that you have the patient's nose closed and that you are keeping his head far enough back.

8. Blow steadily after the first four quick breaths. If you continue too rapidly you will tire yourself and may even feel faint.

(Now read page 14).

Holger Nielsen method

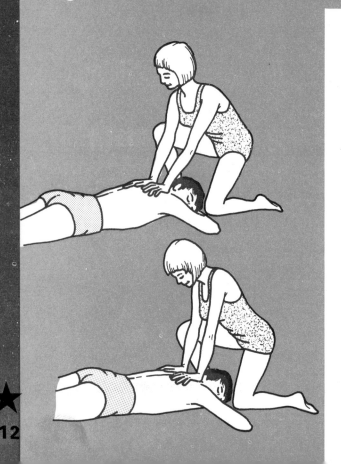

This is used when face injuries make mouth-to-mouth methods undesirable — make sure you have read pages 8 and 9.

1. Position the patient very quickly: on his front, arms over head and elbows bent with both hands (one resting on the other) under his face. His head is to one side with the upper part of the cheek resting on the hands.
2. Position yourself: on one knee close to the patient's forehead; the foot of the other leg near the patient's elbow.
3. Put the "heels" of your hands over patient's shoulder blades at a level corresponding to a line joining the armpits; spread your fingers out over his ribs with your thumbs touching. Rock forward steadily until your arms (kept straight) are about vertical. This compresses the chest and corresponds to expiration.
4. Begin to rock backwards and immediately slip your hands to the patient's armpits and along the upper arms to grasp them on the shoulder side of the elbows. Continue the backwards rock, slightly raising his elbows until you are about vertical and feel resistance and tension at his shoulder. The move has expanded the chest and corresponds to inspiration.
5. Drop the elbows and go back at once to move 3. The cycle of moves 3, 4 and 5 is repeated rhythmically, taking about 6 seconds for the whole movement.

important safeguards in the Holger Nielsen method

1. Make sure that the patient's nose and mouth are not obstructed and that his mouth is near the ground.

3. The steady rocking movement of your body will provide all the pressures needed. Do not bend the elbows. Do not push down. Do not let your arms go beyond the vertical. With small patients reduce the pressure.

4. Let your hands reach the patient's elbows as you begin to rock backwards but are still leaning forward.
Do not bend your elbows.
Do not rock too far back (which is tiring and inefficient).

(Now read page 14).

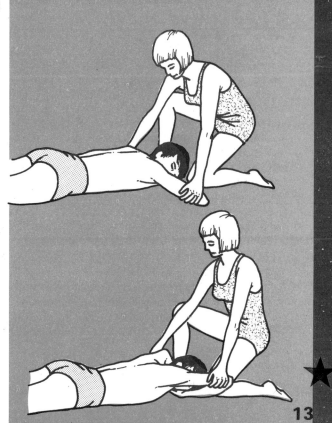

13

further notes on artificial respiration

1. **No time must be lost.** Every second counts.
2. **Get the patient to hospital as quickly as possible.** But do not leave him to send a message; use a bystander.

    Ask the ambulance to bring an oxygen set; the attendants will know how to use it. Artificial respiration must continue while the patient is being put on the stretcher and during the ambulance journey.
3. **For how long do you give artificial respiration?**

    There is no fixed time when you can stop. If you tire and others are present explain to one of them how you are working; let him come alongside and take over the task from you. Artificial respiration must not stop until the patient begins to breathe for himself or a doctor says that the patient has died.
4. **If the patient is a child** you will need less force in blowing or pressing than for an adult. Do not do more than is necessary to get the chest moving. You may find it more convenient to seal your lips round both nose and mouth.
5. **You may blow through the patient's nose** instead of his mouth. In this case seal your lips on the patient's face round his nose, closing his mouth with your thumb.
6. **Get a bystander to cover the body and legs** of the patient with coats or blankets. But do not stop artificial respiration while this is being done.
7. **When the patient begins to breathe for himself** CONTINUE TO WATCH HIM CAREFULLY. He may stop again and need more help. Place him on his side as he may vomit (see page 49).

The term Emergency Resuscitation involves artificial respiration, also sometimes external heart compression (see Appendix), the latter, however, being carried out only by an experienced first-aider.

ELECTRIC SHOCK

DO NOT TOUCH THE PATIENT WHILST HE IS STILL IN CONTACT WITH THE ELECTRICITY OR YOU WILL RISK BECOMING ELECTROCUTED YOURSELF.

1. STOP THE CURRENT at once by **switching off** or by **pulling out the plug**.
   If this is impossible, knock the patient's limb clear of the contact with something which is **dry** and which will not conduct electricity; wood, folded newspaper or rubber. Do NOT use metal which is a conductor. When you do this stand on a dry surface.
2. The patient's breathing or heart beat may have stopped. If necessary start emergency resuscitation (see pages 8 & 14).

important

Electricity from overhead cables or from some factory installations is far more powerful than home electricity. With these it is impossible to give first aid and very dangerous to try before the authorities have fully stopped the current. Until then keep back twenty yards.

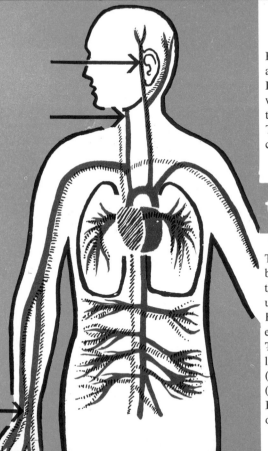

Blood is pumped from the heart through **arteries** to every part of the body and returns to the heart in **veins.**

It carries oxygen (from the lungs), nourishment (from digested food) and warmth. It also takes away waste matter such as carbon dioxide, releasing this in the lungs while taking up fresh oxygen.

The adult heart normally beats 60 to 80 times a minute. In children this can be faster, up to 100 times a minute.

the pulse

This is a throb, felt in an artery, corresponding to each beat of the heart. It can best be found at the wrist on the same side as the thumb, where an artery runs closely under the skin.

Feel with the tips of three fingers just above the outer edge of the crease between palm and forearm.

The pulse can also be felt at other places where arteries lie under the skin, for example:

(a) at the side of the neck (the carotid artery).

(b) immediately in front of the ear.

By practice you will learn to recognise the normal pulse, or that which is faster or weaker than usual.

briefly and diagrammatically the circulation works this way

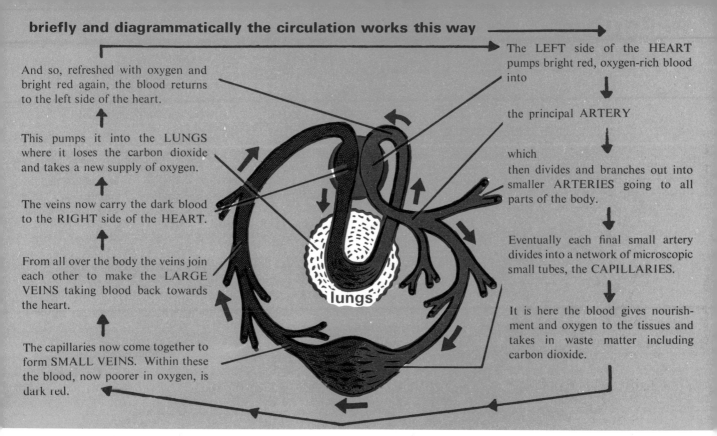

And so, refreshed with oxygen and bright red again, the blood returns to the left side of the heart.

This pumps it into the LUNGS where it loses the carbon dioxide and takes a new supply of oxygen.

The veins now carry the dark blood to the RIGHT side of the HEART.

From all over the body the veins join each other to make the LARGE VEINS taking blood back towards the heart.

The capillaries now come together to form SMALL VEINS. Within these the blood, now poorer in oxygen, is dark red.

lungs

The LEFT side of the HEART pumps bright red, oxygen-rich blood into

the principal ARTERY

which then divides and branches out into smaller ARTERIES going to all parts of the body.

Eventually each final small artery divides into a network of microscopic small tubes, the CAPILLARIES.

It is here the blood gives nourishment and oxygen to the tissues and takes in waste matter including carbon dioxide.

ARTERIES lead blood from the heart to the capillaries.   VEINS lead blood from the capillaries back to the heart.   **17**

It is at the CAPILLARIES that the blood keeps the body alive by supplying nourishment and oxygen and by taking away waste matter.

Slight bleeding will usually stop if you treat it as a wound (see page 24).

SEVERE BLEEDING, FLOWING FAST AND FREELY, MUST BE STOPPED AT ONCE.

1. **Press directly with your thumb and fingers** on to or around the wound. If necessary grasp and hold its edges firmly together. You may have to keep up this pressure until bleeding has been controlled and a dressing is available. Quick control is most important.

2. **Seat the patient** or lay him down.

3. **Raise the bleeding part** if possible. This must not be done if a fractured bone is suspected.

4. **Press the dressing** over the wound. Keep it well in position, cover it with a thick pad and bandage it firmly (see page 78).

   Make sure that the dressing extends well beyond the area of the wound.

   Improvised dressings and bandages in an emergency can be made from clean handkerchiefs or towels (see page 25).

5. **If bleeding continues** and blood oozes through the bandage do not remove the original dressing. Add more dressings and pads and bandage firmly.

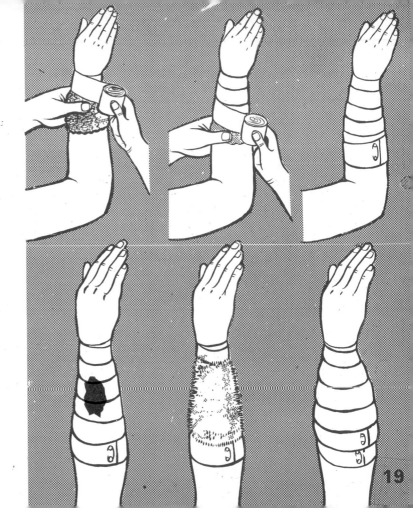

cut in palm of hand with severe bleeding-no foreign bodies in wound

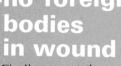

7 Finally support the arm in a triangular sling. (See Page 82)

1 Raise the hand and try to stop the bleeding with pressure of the thumb.

2 Cover the wound with a dressing. Place a small firm pad over the dressing. Close the fingers tightly over the pad.

3 Apply a narrow bandage. (see page 80)

4 Cross its ends over the base of the thumb; pull the bandage tight.

5 Now pass the ends round the base of the little finger and pull the bandage tight.

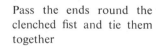

6 Pass the ends round the clenched fist and tie them together

20

bleeding from a tooth socket

This may happen after the tooth has had to be removed by a dentist.

1. Sit the patient up.
2. Put a small piece of lint or gauze firmly on (but not deep in) the socket. It has to be big enough to project above the level of the remaining teeth. The patient now bites hard on the pad for at least 10 minutes.

He can help himself by putting his elbow on the table and raising his jaw in his cupped hand.

bleeding from the outer part of the ear

Control it by pressing your fingers on a dressing or other clean material placed over the cut.

bleeding from inside the ear

Do NOT put anything in the ear.

Do NOT plug with wool.

Cover the whole of the ear with a clean dressing which you bandage to the head.

bleeding from the nose

1. Tell him to pinch the soft (lower) part of the nose firmly for ten minutes.
2. Sit the patient in front of an open window with the head bent slightly forward.
3. Tell him to spit out any excess fluid in his mouth, as swallowing may disturb any blood clot.
4. For some hours after, the patient should avoid handling or blowing his nose lest he start the bleeding again.
5. Undo any tight clothing at the neck.

If bleeding from the ear or nose has followed a blow on the head this might mean a fractured skull (see page 51). Lay the patient down with the head slightly raised and, in the case of the ear, turned towards the bleeding side. He should be sent to hospital as soon as possible.

bleeding from varicose veins

A varicose vein is an enlarged vein on the surface of a leg. If it bursts the bleeding can be severe.

treatment

1. At once cover it and press hard with the hand, until you can get a dressing.
2. Lay the patient down with the leg raised.
3. Remove any garter.
4. Cover the bleeding point with a dressing and pad and bandage very firmly.
5. Get a doctor or send to hospital.

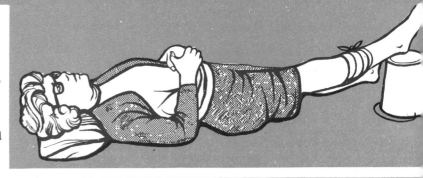

internal bleeding

Hidden bleeding can take place inside the body and not show on the surface:
(a) In severe injuries which damage large blood vessels anywhere in the body.
(b) In some illnesses which may cause sudden bleeding inside the abdomen or chest.
THE ALERT FIRST-AIDER WILL SUSPECT THIS DANGEROUS STATE FROM:
    A large degree of swelling at an injured part.
    Sometimes great pain in the chest or abdomen.
    The rapid development of all the signs of shock (see page 26).

treatment

1. Absolute rest.
2. All anti-shock measures (see page 27).
3. Rapidly obtain medical aid and transport carefully to hospital without delay.

BRUISING

This is bleeding under the skin from an injury which may or may not break the skin. A tender lump or swelling quickly forms and the area becomes blue/black after a short time.

1. Put the part at rest.

2. Apply a cold compress.

A "black eye" is a bruise. As it may involve damage to the eye or skull it is best seen by a doctor.

SPLINTERS

If the splinter is sticking out it can be removed with clean tweezers. Otherwise it should be left to a doctor or nurse. It is so easy to push the splinter further in and make it more difficult to remove.

to make a cold compress

1. Take a piece of lint, flannel, linen, a large handkerchief or thin towel.

2. Fold it to the size required and soak it in cold water.

3. Squeeze it out until it stops dripping.

4. Apply to the injured part. Leave uncovered or secure with open weave material like gauze, as evaporation helps the cooling effect.

5. Keep it moist and cool by dripping on water as necessary.

23

A wound is a break in the skin. This allows:

(a) **Blood to escape.** Serious bleeding must be dealt with at once (see page 18).

(b) **Germs to enter.** Germs are too small to be seen without a microscope, and are carried by flies and unwashed hands. If they settle in a wound they grow and cause infection. When dressing a wound you must have everything as clean as possible.

Gauze in layers is commonly used as a dressing.

1. Seat the patient.
2. Wash your hands thoroughly.
3. Collect all the equipment you need. Place it on a clean towel or handkerchief. Avoid coughing over wound or equipment.
4. Remove clothing from the injured part only, if necessary.
5. Protect the wound temporarily by keeping it covered with a clean swab; gently clean around it with soap and water. Do this with swabs of wool or gauze in separate strokes, moving away from the wound and using a fresh piece for each stroke. Do not disturb any blood clots as this may start the bleeding again. A small wound may be washed with clean water under a running tap.
6. Remove any loose foreign matter (glass, metal, gravel). But do NOT try to remove anything which is EMBEDDED in the wound.
7. Touching the material only by the edges, cut the gauze with clean scissors to a size large enough not only to cover the wound fully, but also to extend over the surrounding skin. Hold it by the corner and place it over the wound.

8. Cover with cotton wool and bandage gently, but firmly enough to make sure that the dressing does not slip later. An adhesive dressing may be used for a small wound. **Prepared sterile dressings** are often used in place of gauze, wool and bandage. **(see page 79)**

If an embedded object projects from the wound (a piece of glass or metal) prevent your bandage from pressing on it by using a ring pad (see page 81) or by building up cotton wool round it, **over the dressing,** before bandaging.

9. Rest the injured part.
10. If necessary take anti-shock measures (see page 27).

GRAZES

A graze follows rubbing or scraping the surface of the skin.
Wash it gently to clear the surface dirt, using swabs of wool or gauze.
Cover and dress it as a wound.

emergency dressings

If you have no dressings use what is available. A clean handkerchief, small towel or pillow case will do. After washing your hands, hold it up by the corners and let it fall open. Then refold it to the size you need so that what was its inside, unexposed, surface is now on the outside. Hold it carefully, by the edges and the corners and do not let the new surface touch your hands or the table before it is put on the wound.
A clean scarf, towel, handkerchief or lady's stocking can be used as a bandage.

SHOCK

THIS IS A DANGEROUS STATE OF COLLAPSE WHICH MAY DEVELOP AFTER SEVERE INJURY.

It must not be confused with a state of emotion or fear, or with simple fainting.

its causes
It may follow: Heavy **bleeding** including internal bleeding.
Severe **burns.**
Large **fractures**.
Extensive **wounds** and **bruises**.
Fluid loss from very heavy **diarrhoea** and **vomiting.**

its appearance
When the patient is shocked:
He loses **colour** and is very pale or grey.
His **skin** is cold and moist with sweat.
His **pulse** is weak and fast.
His **breathing** is fast but shallow. In severe cases however it may
become gasping.
He may be **restless** at first and later may go into **coma.**

THIS ALARMING STATE NEEDS URGENT HOSPITAL TREATMENT.

Shock DEVELOPS after injury. It may steadily worsen and lead to death.
The first-aider's aim is to PREVENT shock developing after injury or accident.
This must be done even if the patient appears to be in good condition.

how to prevent shock

GIVE THE TREATMENT NECESSARY FOR THE INJURY

1. Stop any bleeding immediately.

2. Move the patient as little as possible. Lay him down. Put something soft under his head and raise his legs (if they are not fractured) above the level of his head. This can be done with folded coats or rugs. If he is in bed raise the foot end by suitable props underneath. Turn his head to one side.

3. Loosen any tight clothing round the neck, chest and waist.

4 Protect if necessary with blankets, rugs or coats, under as well as over the body or in hot climates protect from the sun.

5. Stay with the patient and do all you can to relieve anxiety and to reassure.

6. Obtain medical help (or ambulance) rapidly.

> DO NOT give anything to eat or drink to a patient –
> who is unconscious
> who has a suspected internal abdominal or chest injury
> who is shortly to be given an anaesthetic

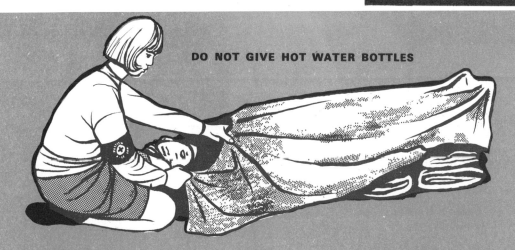

DO NOT GIVE HOT WATER BOTTLES

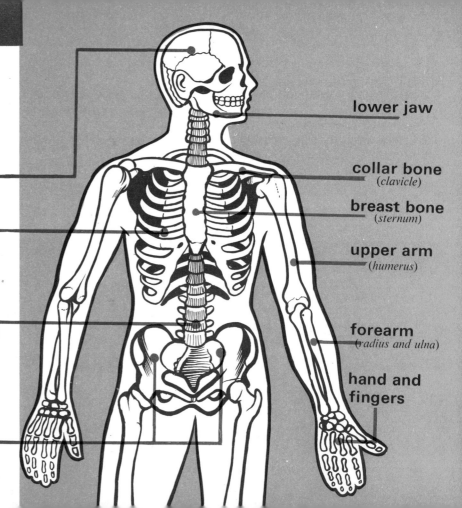

The bones give shape and firmness to the body and provide levers over which muscles work. They protect important organs such as the brain, the heart and the lungs.

skull

Several bones fixed together which protect the brain.

ribs

12 pairs of curved flat bones join the spine to the breastbone. The chest cavity so formed protects the lungs and the heart.

spine

This consists of a row of bones (vertebrae) which enclose and protect the spinal cord of nerves. They are separated from each other by cartilage discs. This arrangement allows movement of the back and neck.

pelvis

This consists of two haunch bones and the bottom of the spine. It provides sockets for the thigh bones.

lower jaw

collar bone
(*clavicle*)

breast bone
(*sternum*)

upper arm
(*humerus*)

forearm
(*radius and ulna*)

hand and fingers

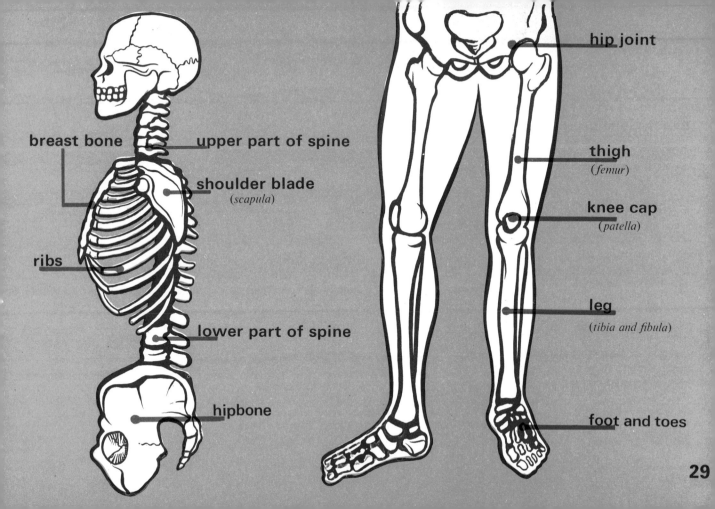

breast bone

upper part of spine

shoulder blade
(*scapula*)

ribs

lower part of spine

hipbone

hip joint

thigh
(*femur*)

knee cap
(*patella*)

leg
(*tibia and fibula*)

foot and toes

29

FRACTURES

A break of a bone is called a FRACTURE. It can be caused by:

direct violence

The break occurs where the blow falls. *Examples: car wheel running over leg, hammer hitting a finger, man falling from ladder.*

indirect violence

The break occurs some distance away from the impact. *Examples: collar bone fracture due to fall on hand with outstretched arm, top of thigh-bone fractured from heavy fall on heel.*

muscular action

The break is caused by a violent muscular contraction, pulling the bone. *Example: The knee-cap when avoiding a fall backwards.*

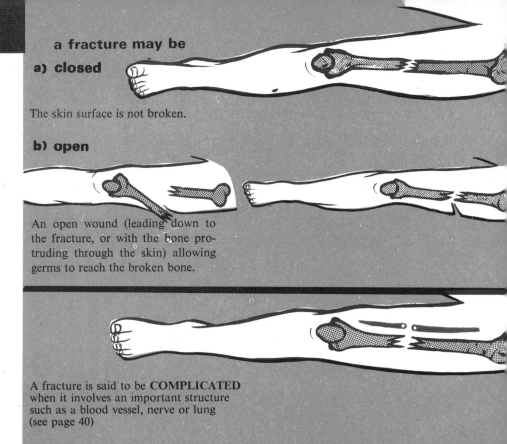

a fracture may be

a) closed

The skin surface is not broken.

b) open

An open wound (leading down to the fracture, or with the bone protruding through the skin) allowing germs to reach the broken bone.

A fracture is said to be **COMPLICATED** when it involves an important structure such as a blood vessel, nerve or lung (see page 40)

symptoms and signs of fractures

Pain.
The injured part cannot be moved normally.
It may have an unnatural shape or position.
Swelling and sometimes bruising.

(all of these may not be present in every case).

rules of treatment

IF IN DOUBT TREAT AS A FRACTURE.

Aim to prevent further damage by avoiding unnecessary movement of the broken bone.

1. **Treat the patient on the spot** (unless he is in danger there). Tell him not to move.
2. **Cover any open wound.**
3. Handle gently and steady the injured limb.
4. **Immobilise the injured part.** Use bandages and slings **and tie it firmly to the patient's own body;** for example tying an injured leg to the other leg, or an arm to the chest. Splints, if required, can be improvised: pieces of wood, newspapers rolled and tied together.
   Bandage so that the joint above and the joint below the fracture are both immobilised.
5. **Use plenty of padding** (cotton wool, towels, dressings, small items of clothing) especially between the skin surfaces and whenever you use a splint.
6. **Treat to prevent shock.**
7. **Get medical aid.**

Make the knots on the uninjured side. Tie bandages firmly but not too tight.

to test circulation in the arm

Press the patient's fingernail so that the nail turns white. When pressure is released, the nail should quickly become pink again. showing that the blood has returned. The bandage is too tight if the nail remains white or blue, or if the fingers are cold.

fractured ribs

symptom Pain in the chest gets worse when taking a deep breath.

Support the arm on the injured side in an arm sling (see page 81).
For complicated fracture see page 40.

fractured collarbone

This may follow a fall on the outstretched arm which carries the force
of the blow up to the shoulder region.

symptoms Pain in the shoulder.
The arm is helpless.
The patient may bend his head towards
the injured side and may support the
elbow of the injured side with the other
hand to relieve weight and muscle
pull on the collar bone.

1. Encircle each shoulder with a narrow
   fold bandage which passes under the
   armpit and is tied at the back with a
   reef knot.
2. Place a soft pad in position between
   the shoulder blades.
3. While the patient presses his shoulders
   back as much as he can, tie together
   the long free ends of each bandage or
   use a third bandage to keep a firm pull
   on the braced shoulders.
4. Support the arm on the injured side
   in a triangular sling.

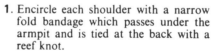

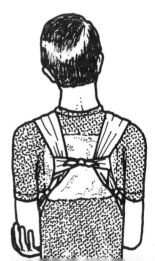

32

symptoms and signs

The usual fracture features: pain, loss of power, deformity, swelling, bruising.

The patient may support the injured part with the forearm across his chest.

A fractured hand may show much bruising and swelling.

1. Gently bend the elbow to bring the forearm if possible straight across the chest.
2. Protect the injured part by placing soft padding between it and the chest.
3. Support in an arm sling.
4. **Where there is a long difficult journey,** secure the broken arm to the chest with a broad bandage,

fractured hand

1. Gently bend the elbow.
2. Protect the hand with soft padding.
3. Support in a triangular sling (see page 82).
4. The arm is now held in this position by a broad bandage round the chest and over the sling.

but note carefully

An injured ELBOW must not be bent if this causes pain and is difficult.

(a) If it is found bent, treat as a fracture of the upper arm.

(b) If it is found straight, tie the arm to the side of the body with three broad bandages:
Round the upper arm and body.
Below the elbow and round the body.
Over the wrist and round the thigh.

Move the patient by stretcher.

33

fractured thigh and leg

symptoms and signs   Pain, loss of power, deformity, swelling, bruising.

In **thigh bone** fractures the limb MAY roll sideways with the toes pointing outwards.

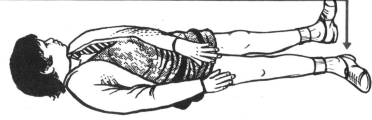

When the journey is short and smooth

1. Slowly and gently try to bring the lower limbs in line with each other.
2. Place soft pads between the thighs, knees and ankles.
3. Tie the feet and ankles together with a figure-of-eight bandage, (Bandage No. 1).
4. Bandage the knees together, (Bandage No. 2).
   CAUTION: If attempt to align the lower limbs causes too much pain do not persist. Maintain the position of broken limb with pillows or bandages.

when there is a long and difficult journey

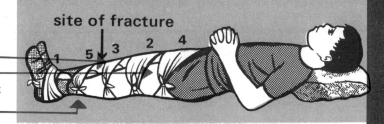

Add three more bandages:
Round the legs. (Bandage No. 3).
Round the thighs. (Bandage No. 4).
Just below the site of the fracture (shown here as just below the calf). (Bandage No. 5).

IF SPLINTS ARE AVAILABLE OR CAN BE IMPROVISED:

When the LEG is fractured:

1. Use a well padded splint between the limbs.
2. Apply five bandages as above.

When the THIGH is fractured:

1. Apply the padded splint between the limbs.
2. In addition apply a long padded splint on the outer side of the injured limb and up to just below the armpit. Secure this with two broad bandages:
   Round the chest
   (Bandage a).
   Round the hips. (Bandage b).
3. Finish off with the 5 bandages as above, the last one being placed below the site of the fracture.

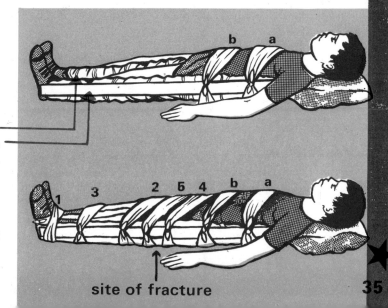

fractured foot

1. Remove footwear (including socks or stockings); you may have to cut them.
2. Dress any wound present.
3. Put a padded splint from heel to toe along the sole of the foot, as described below.
4. Tie with a figure-of-eight bandage. Begin with the centre of the bandage under the foot. Cross it over the foot and carry each end round the back of the ankle. Cross them once more over the front and tie off under the foot.
5. Raise and support the foot in a comfortable position.

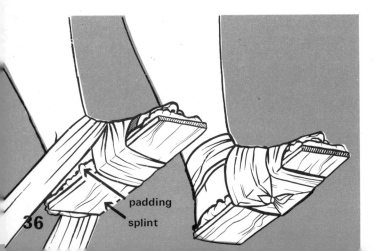

padding

splint

fractured patella (knee cap)

The knee cap may be broken by direct force and also (rarely) may be snapped in two by the strong pull of the powerful muscle leading into it from the front of the thigh.

symptoms Swelling at the front of the knee. Pain which gets worse if the patient tries to move the leg.

1. Lie the patient down with head and shoulders raised and supported.
2. Place a well padded splint under the leg from buttock to beyond the heel.
3. Secure the leg to the splint by:
   (a) a figure-of-eight bandage round the ankle and foot.
   (b) a broad bandage round the thigh.
   (c) a broad bandage round the lower leg.
4. Keep the limb in a comfortable raised position.

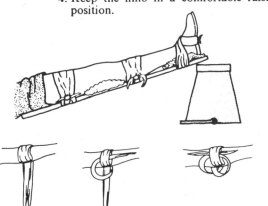

fractured lower jaw

symptoms and signs

Pain on movement.
Cannot speak or swallow easily.
Teeth appear irregular.
Bleeding or dribbling from the mouth.

1. Remove any loose objects in the mouth, broken teeth or dentures.
2. Tell the patient to lean forward so that any blood or excess saliva can flow out.
3. Support the jaw by a soft pad held in the palm of the hand — if he is fit enough the patient can do this himself.

4. Support can be maintained by any improvised wide bandage (e.g. a woman's stocking) brought upwards from under the jaw and tied on top of the head.
   If the patient appears likely to vomit remove the bandage and support his jaw.
If he is seriously injured and lying down or unconscious, he is kept in the recovery position (see page 47).

fractured pelvis
symptoms

Pain in the hip, groin or loin regions.
Standing is painful or impossible.

Lay the patient on his back.
Allow him to place his feet in the most comfortable position.
If he wishes to bend his knees support them with a folded blanket or coat underneath.

Sometimes a complicated fracture damages the bladder and the patient may feel that he wishes to pass water. Were he to do so the damage would worsen. He should be told not to pass water if he can avoid it.

when there is a long and difficult journey

1. Apply two overlapping broad bandages firmly round the pelvis and hips.
2. Put padding between knees and ankles.
3. Tie the feet and ankles together with a figure-of-eight bandage.
4. Apply a broad bandage round the knees.

symptoms and signs

Pain in the back or neck.
Sometimes loss of power or of feeling in feet or hands.

A fractured spine involves the risk of severely damaging nerves and causing paralysis if moved carelessly, especially if the back or neck is allowed to bend forwards or be twisted.

if medical help is easily available

DO NOT MOVE THE PATIENT.

Tell him to keep still, lying down.
Cover him with a coat or blanket and make him comfortable.

if medical help is not available

The patient must be taken carefully by stretcher to hospital without bending or twisting his back or neck.

Gently straighten the legs. Put pads between the thighs, knees and ankles. Tie the ankles and feet together with a figure-of-eight bandage. Tie bandages round the thighs and round the knees.

ONE FIRST-AIDER SUPPORTS THE HEAD AND ANOTHER THE FEET, UNTIL THE PATIENT IS ON A STRETCHER.

A blanket rolled lengthwise for half its width is placed with the roll alongside the patient. He is now SLOWLY AND GENTLY turned in one piece on his side and the roll is placed close to his back. He is now turned over the roll onto his opposite side on the blanket. The blanket is unrolled out flat. The patient is turned gently onto his back on it.

A stretcher is brought to the feet of the patient (a canvas type stretcher must be stiffened with short boards placed across it).
Place pads on the stretcher to support the patient's neck, small of back, knees and ankles.
Roll the two edges of the blanket up against the patient's sides.
The blanket (kept taut by grasping its rolled edges) is raised just enough to allow the stretcher to be slid underneath him.
The patient is gently and evenly lowered onto it.

UNTIL THIS IS COMPLETED THE TWO FIRST-AIDERS AT THE HEAD AND FEET HAVE KEPT THESE PARTS RIGIDLY IN LINE WITH THE BODY.

At least four, and sometimes six, first-aiders are needed.

COMPLICATED FRACTURES

A complicated fracture is one in which an important body structure is damaged by the broken bone.

The first-aider should always think of this possibility whenever he treats a fracture.

treatment

Patients with complicated fractures should be placed in the lying position.

In the case of the ribs the patient should be turned **towards** the injured side with his head and shoulders raised. Any open chest wound 'sucking' air in and out should promptly and firmly be covered with a large dressing.

REMEMBER THAT MOVEMENT OF A BROKEN BONE OR CARELESS HANDLING COULD CAUSE THE COMPLICATION.

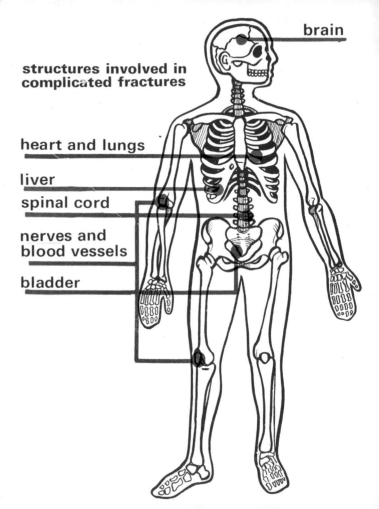

structures involved in complicated fractures

brain

heart and lungs

liver

spinal cord

nerves and blood vessels

bladder

JOINTS

Joints are formed where two or more bones meet (ARTICULATE).
Different joints have their own types of movement.

The bones are held together by elastic-like cuffs (LIGAMENTS).
Together these ligaments form a covering (CAPSULE) surrounding the joint.

Lining the capsule is a thin membrane which produces a fluid
to "oil" the joint.

The adjacent surfaces of the bones are covered with a gristle (CARTILAGE)
whose smoothness allows the bones to move easily.

hip joint

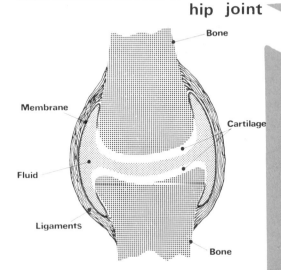

Bone

Membrane

Cartilage

Fluid

Ligaments

Bone

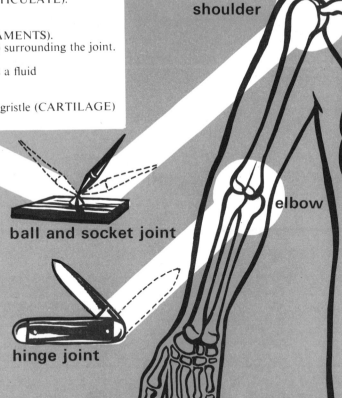

shoulder

elbow

ball and socket joint

hinge joint

41

This is due to a twist which tears or stretches the ligaments, but does not displace the bones.

symptoms and signs Pain which worsens on trying to move the limb. Swelling round the joint.

warning

These features are similar to those of a fracture.
A fracture near a joint is also likely to cause a sprain.
A swollen joint may mask a fracture.

if in doubt treat as a fracture

1. Rest the joint in the most comfortable position.
2. Either (a) apply support; surround the joint and the area above and below with a thick layer of cotton wool. Bandage firmly with a roller or narrow triangular bandage.

Over this apply a second layer of wool and again bandage firmly.

or, (b) apply a cold compress (see page 23).

In the case of the wrist, elbow or shoulder joint, support it in an arm sling.

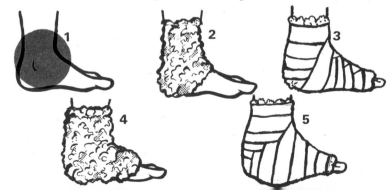

dislocation of a joint

This is caused by a twist or severe wrench which displaces the bones and also tears the ligaments.

1. Support the part in the most comfortable position, using plenty of padding.
2. Get medical aid quickly.

DO NOT TRY TO PUT THE BONE BACK INTO POSITION, MOVE THE LIMB AS LITTLE AS POSSIBLE.

symptoms and signs

Pain.
Inability to move the joint normally.
Sometimes numbness down the limb due to the stretching of nerves.
Deformity.
Swelling.

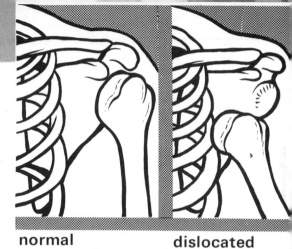

normal   dislocated

displaced cartilage of the knee

Two pads of cartilage lie between the bones of the knee joint. If the knee is wrenched suddenly (as in playing games) the cartilage may be torn and displaced.

The knee is painful and cannot be fully straightened. It may be swollen. Treat as for dislocation.

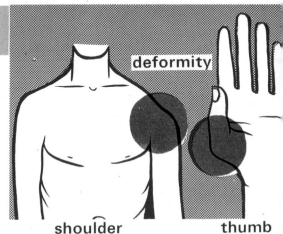

deformity

shoulder   thumb

43

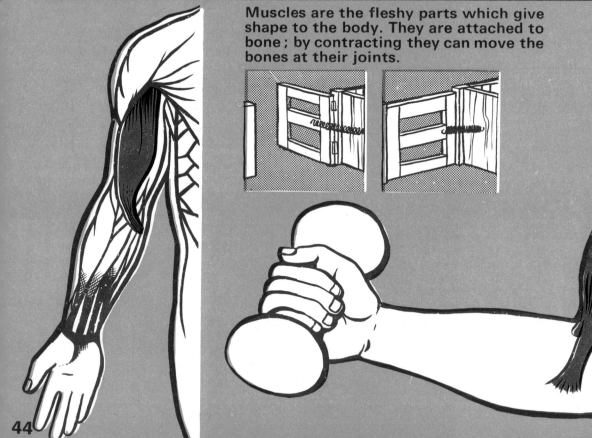

Muscles are the fleshy parts which give shape to the body. They are attached to bone; by contracting they can move the bones at their joints.

44

A muscle can be STRAINED or RUPTURED by the over-stretching or tearing of some of its fibres. These accidents can happen by sudden severe exertion or in handling heavy weights.

symptoms and signs

Sudden pain, worse on movement. Sometimes swelling and bruising.

Support the injured part with a firm bandage.

This consists of:

THE BRAIN in the head, the 'controlling headquarters' of life in all the body.

THE SPINAL CORD which extends from the base of the brain and runs down the neck and back, inside the vertebral column (spine).

THE NERVES issuing from the brain and from the spinal cord, carrying messages to and from all parts of the body.

The brain is like the switchboard of a large telephone exchange. The spinal cord represents a collection of cables carrying wires to different areas of a town. The nerves are like the separate wires dispersed to individual telephones.

Damage anywhere in the system could cause loss of feeling or loss of movement (paralysis) in those areas of the body served by the damaged nerves.

The skull protects the brain in the upper part of the head.

The spinal cord is protected by the bones of the vertebral column.

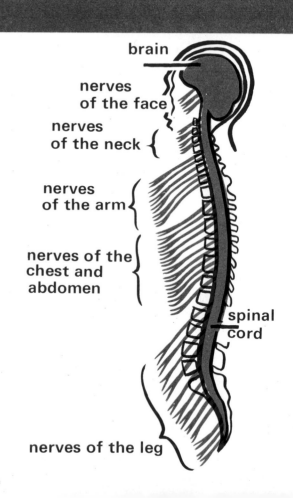

brain

nerves of the face

nerves of the neck

nerves of the arm

nerves of the chest and abdomen

spinal cord

nerves of the leg

space occupied by brain in the skull

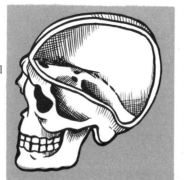

The brain rests on the **base of the skull,** which lies at the level of the ears, eyes and nose.

UNCONSCIOUSNESS

Unconsciousness is always due to the brain not working properly. This may be caused by:

Lack of oxygen in the blood supply, as occurs when breathing is interfered with.

Shortage of blood supply to the brain; fainting and shock.

Injury to the brain (see page 52).

Disease of the brain.

position for unconsciousness (the recovery position)

This prevents the patient's tongue from falling back into the throat and allows fluids to drain from the mouth.

1. If necessary give Emergency Respiration. (see pages 8-14)

2. Stop any serious bleeding at once, except from the ears (see page 51).

3. Put the patient in the POSITION FOR UNCONSCIOUSNESS (the RECOVERY POSITION).

4. Clear the mouth of any obstruction including froth, blood or vomit. Remove any false teeth and keep safely (too often false teeth get broker or lost through careless handling).

5. Loosen clothing at the neck, chest and waist.

6. Place blankets or coats above and below the patient.

7. Send for doctor.

DO NOT GIVE ANYTHING BY MOUTH.
DO NOT LEAVE THE PATIENT.

Patient lying on one side.

Head tilted slightly backwards.

The leg and arm of the side on which he is lying are stretched out behind him.

The other arm and leg are bent in front of him with the hip, knee and the elbow at about a right angle.

47

FAINTING

Before fainting the patient feels unsteady, giddy.
His sight may blur.
He feels cold and clammy.
He starts to sweat.
On fainting the patient becomes unconscious.
His face is pale.
His pulse is slow and weak.

1. Lay him down in the fresh air if possible.
2. Raise his legs above the level of the head.
3. Loosen tight clothing at the neck, chest and waist.
4. **When he has recovered consciousness,** give him sips of cold water.

If he cannot lie down (seated in a crowded hall), put his he
down between his knees.

CONVULSIONS IN YOUNG CHILDREN

These may be due to brain disorders, a raised temperature,
digestive upset, fright or temper.
THE CHILD BECOMES STIFF AND ARCHES HIS BACK.
HIS LIMBS MAY TWITCH.
His face becomes red or blue and the eyes roll up.

1. Loosen tight clothing.
2. Wipe any froth from the mouth.
3. If he has a high temperature, reduce it by tepid sponging.
4. Cover him lightly in a blanket and put in the recovery position.
5. Send for a doctor.

(See also EPILEPSY page 54
and HEAT STROKE page 63).

FRACTURED SKULL

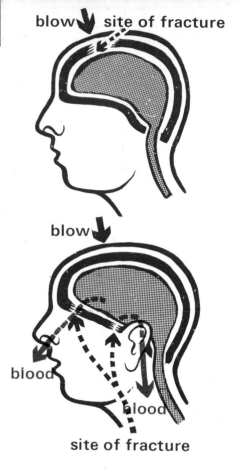

A blow on the top or side of the head can fracture the skull:

At the point which received the blow. The scalp here will be bruised and swollen and may be cut. The possibility of a fracture beneath it must be thought of.

At the base of the skull on which the brain lies, the force of the blow having reached there round the bone. Following this fracture, blood may escape from an ear or through the nose (see page 21).

1. Lay the patient down in the position for unconsciousness (see page 49).
2. With a clean dressing cover any wound of the scalp or bleeding ear to prevent infection which might spread to the brain through the fracture.
3. Lay the patient on the same side as the bleeding ear to allow blood to run out. Do not plug the ear as this would increase the risk of infection.
4. Protect the patient with rugs or coats above and below him.
5. Get a doctor or send the patient to hospital.

BRAIN INJURY

Blows on the head can damage the brain in two main ways: CONCUSSION and COMPRESSION.

concussion

This results from a 'shaking-up' of the brain.

The patient is unconscious for a short time. Pulse is weak and breathing shallow. In very severe cases no breathing may be detected.

As he recovers the patient may be dazed and may vomit. He may not remember events just before the accident.

1. If necessary give artificial respiration.
2. Treat as for unconsciousness (see page 49).
3. When he recovers consciousness keep him at rest. He must not be allowed to take up his game or work again until seen by a doctor.

compression

This is due to pressure on the brain from a fracture of the skull with the bone depressed or the escape of blood from a broken vessel within the skull.

The patient has a headache.
He becomes drowsy and then unconscious.
Pulse and breathing may be slow.
There may be twitching of limbs or convulsions.
The pupils of the eyes may be of different sizes.

1. Treat as for unconsciousness (see page 49).
2. Get a doctor or ambulance urgently.

important
A patient with concussion may recover consciousness and after an interval develop compression.
All patients with head injuries may have other injuries elsewhere and these should be carefully looked for.

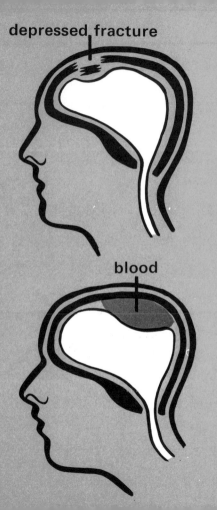

depressed fracture

blood

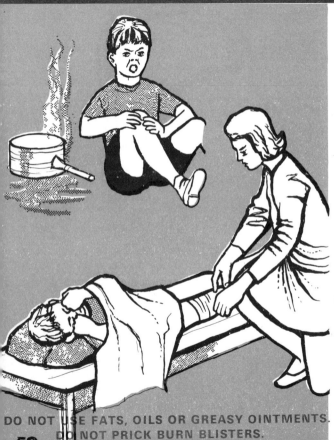

BURNS are caused by **dry** heat—fire or electricity or contact with hot objects.

SCALDS are caused by **moist** heat—steam, boiling water or hot fat.

CHEMICAL BURNS are caused by **corrosives**—strong acids and alkalis.

treatment for a burn or scald

1. Stop the spread of heat and reduce pain and swelling by immediately flooding, or preferably immersing, the burnt part in clean cold water if available. This should be continued for at least 10 minutes or until pain is relieved.

2. Burnt clothing (which has already been sterilised by the burn) should not be disturbed. However, clothing soaked in boiling water should be carefully removed.

3. Remove anything which may cause constriction (rings or bracelets).

4. **Lightly cover with a dressing and bandage. A burnt face may be covered by a gauze mask with a hole for breathing cut in it.**

5. Take anti-shock measures.

6. Get a doctor or send the patient to hospital without delay.

   If there is a delay (half an hour or more) in getting the patient to hospital give him water to drink, but it must be sipped very slowly and be no more than a small cupful every fifteen minutes.

for a corrosive chemical injury

At once flood the burned area with copious running water, protecting the unaffected areas, e.g. an uninjured eye.

Remove the contaminated clothing (avoid contaminating yourself).

Treat as a wound (see page 24).

DO NOT USE FATS, OILS OR GREASY OINTMENTS. DO NOT PRICK BURN BLISTERS.

clothes catching fire

Put out the flames with cold water or any other non-inflammable fluid if immediately at hand.

Otherwise smother the flames by laying the patient down and wrapping a blanket, rug or coat tightly round him.

Tear off smouldering clothes by seizing them in a non-burning area.

SEVERE BURNS, ESPECIALLY THOSE INVOLVING A LARGE AMOUNT OF THE BODY'S SURFACE, CAUSE EXTENSIVE SHOCK WHICH MAY BE MORE DANGEROUS TO LIFE THAN THE BURNS THEMSELVES. THE PATIENT URGENTLY NEEDS HOSPITAL TREATMENT.

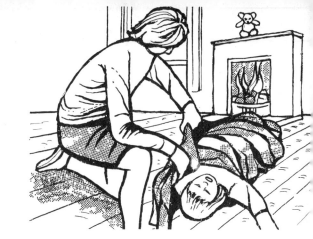

scalded or burnt throat or mouth   sunburn

This may result from drinking extremely hot fluid or corrosive poisons, or, in small children, from putting the mouth to the spout of a hot kettle.

The inside of the throat and mouth may swell so much as to interfere with the air flow to and from the lungs.

1. Lie the patient in the recovery position.
2. If he is conscious give cold water to drink or ice to suck.
3. If necessary give artificial respiration.
4. Arrange for urgent transport to hospital.

Serious discomfort and even superficial burns with blister formation and swelling can be caused by the direct rays of the sun, especially near the sea or in mountains.

Treatment:

1. Rest the patient in the shade.
2. Give him fluids to drink.
3. Mild cases may be helped by lotions or creams.
4. If the sunburn is severe seek medical aid.

Prevention:

Prevention is better than cure. Exposure to the sun should be gradual and at first only small portions of the body should be uncovered for short lengths of time.

POISONING

if the patient is unconscious

1. **Is he breathing?** Some poisons stop the action of the lungs and heart. The patient will then need emergency resuscitation. (See pages 10 and 90). It may be necessary first to wash the poison away from the face and mouth.
2. **Is he choking?** Has his tongue fallen back (see page 9)? His throat may need clearing of something obstructing it.
3. Put him in the position for unconsciousness (see page 49).

if the patient is conscious

1. **Watch him carefully.** He may lose consciousness at any time.

2. **Make him vomit repeatedly.** Tickle the back of his throat with two fingers. Better still, give him copious drinks of salt and water (**two tablespoonfuls** of common salt to each tumbler of water, tepid if possible).

danger: leave this step out if the poison is a corrosive or a petroleum product
Strong acid or alkali, if vomited, will cause more harm to the already damaged throat and stomach. With corrosive poisons the lips and mouth may be stained yellow, grey or white. Petroleum products such as kerosene, if vomited are liable to pass into the lungs.

3. **Dilute any poison left in the stomach** by giving to drink, in slow sips, one pint of milk (tepid if possible), or of water if milk is not available.

in all cases of poisoning

1. Send an urgent message for an ambulance or to a doctor. If this is by telephone explain what is the suspected poison and ask for advice on anything else to do while waiting.

2. Do not leave the patient alone.

3. Keep any tablets, medicines or containers. Also save a sample of any vomit for the doctor, or to send to hospital with the patient, as its examination may help diagnosis.

remember
Berries from plants, tablets or medicines swallowed by a child may be poisonous.

HYSTERIA

EPILEPSY

Hysteria may follow anxiety or worries.
The attack takes a little time to develop.

The hysterical patient generally makes a great deal of noise drawing attention to himself.
He does not fall though he may 'collapse' into a fairly safe position.
He may wave his arms and legs wildly or he may move weakly as if to show how ill he feels.

He remains conscious all the time and notices and reacts to the presence of other people.

treatment

1. Reassure him but be very firm.
2. Clear the public and relatives away. An hysterical attack is likely to last longer in front of a sympathetic audience.

Epilepsy is due to disease affecting the brain.
The attack comes on suddenly or with only the briefest warning.
The epileptic is silent (though sometimes the attack may begin with ONE sharp cry).
He falls so suddenly that he is in danger of hurting himself.
At first rigid, with congested face and neck, he soon begins convulsions with jerky shaking of arms and legs. During these he may bite his tongue or empty his bladder or bowels. He may froth at the mouth.
After the convulsions he lies still and unconscious before recovering, dazed and exhausted.

treatment

1. Do not try to stop the jerking.
2. Move the patient clear of nearby furniture or a fire so that he does not injure himself.
3. If you can, remove any false teeth.
4. Put a folded cloth between his jaws to prevent the tongue being bitten.
5. When the convulsions stop, give treatment for unconsciousness (see page 49).

THE ATTACKS OF HYSTERIA AND EPILEPSY DESCRIBED ARE THE USUAL ONES BUT THE PATTERN MAY VARY IN DIFFERENT PERSONS.

IN BOTH THE ABOVE CONDITIONS THE PATIENT SHOULD BE REFERRED TO A DOCTOR.

CRAMP

Cramp is a sudden pain and tightness in the muscles of a limb.

Treat by putting the muscles on the stretch.

FOOT: Straighten the bent toes by pushing them upwards.

CALF: Straighten the patient's knee and pull his foot up at the ankle as far as it will go.

THIGH: Straighten the knee and pull the lower limb forwards.

HAND: Straighten the bent fingers by stretching them backwards.

Someone who has been sweating heavily may suffer from cramp. Give him a drink of water containing a half **teaspoonful** of salt to the pint (two tumblers).

WINDING

Winding is a collapse which may follow a hard blow in the upper part of the abdomen.

1. Place the patient in the position for unconsciousness (see page 49).
2. Loosen any tight clothing at the neck, chest or waist.
3. Gently massage the upper abdomen.

FOREIGN BODIES

in the eye

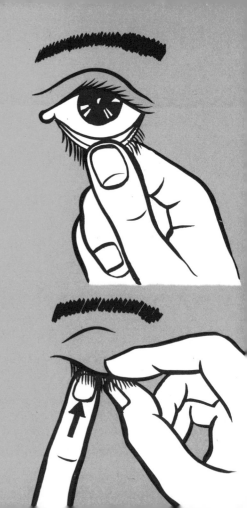

This may be an insect or piece of grit or loose lash.

1. Tell the patient not to rub the eye.
2. Let him blink the eyelid under water if possible. If this is not effective:
3. Sit him in a good light.
4. Wash your hands.
5. While the patient looks up, gently draw the **lower lid** down and out. If the particle is seen on the lower lid, remove it with a moistened wisp of cotton wool or the corner of a clean handkerchief.
6. If the particle is thought to be under the **upper lid,** then while the patient looks down, gently grasp the upper lid and draw it down and out over the lower lid. This may dislodge the foreign body.

If the foreign body cannot easily be wiped away or is embedded, do not try further. Cover the eye lightly with a bandage and send the patient to a doctor or hospital.

in the ear

in the nose

Children sometimes push peas or beads into their ears. Insects may also get in.

1. Do NOT try to poke the object out.
2. If an **insect** is in the ear lay the patient with the affected ear uppermost. Pour in tepid water or cold olive oil and the insect may float out.
3. When **another object** is in the ear turn the patient's head to one side and the object may drop out.

   If you are not successful take the patient to a doctor.

Children sometimes push peas or beans up their nose.

1. Do NOT try to poke the object out.
2. Tell the patient to breathe through the mouth only.
3. Take him to a doctor.

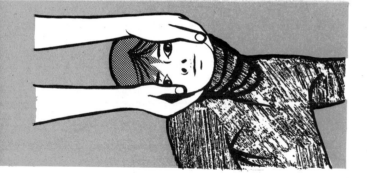

in the throat

If a **fishbone** is lodged in the throat do not attempt to remove it.

Reassure the patient and take to a doctor.

If a **particle of food** is lodged in the throat, see Choking (page 7).

INSECT STINGS

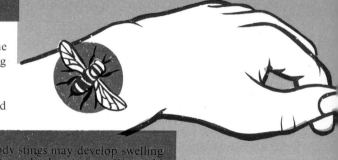

1. If the sting is still in the skin remove it with fine tweezers. Put the tweezers on the part of the sting nearest the skin (to avoid squeezing in any poison left at the other end).
2. Rest the part.
3. Apply an anti-histamine cream if available to reduce the pain and swelling. A cold compress may ease the pain.

Persons stung in the mouth or with severe reactions to many body stings may develop swelling in the gullet which could block breathing and requires immediate medical attention. Give cold drinks or ice to suck. Place him in the recovery position.

BLISTERS FROM RUBBING

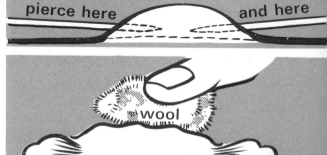

1. Wipe the blister with cotton wool and methylated spirit, or clean it thoroughly with soap and water.
2. Pass a clean needle through the flame of a match or petrol lighter. Do not wipe off the soot or touch it afterwards.
3. Pass the needle through the blister at skin level at two points, as shown.
4. Press the fluid out with a clean dressing and do NOT remove blistered skin.
5. Keep the blister covered with a small dressing until it is healed.

NEVER REMOVE THE BLISTERED SKIN.

SNAKE BITES

In the British Isles

Almost all poisonous snake bites are due to the adder and are generally more painful than dangerous
The adder is about two feet long and its head is broadened. Its colour varies from grey to brick red. The dark markings on the back, occasionally appear as broad spots but much more generally as characteristic zig-zag lines.

1. Reassure the patient.
2. Lay him down at absolute rest.
3. Gently wipe off (or wash away with soapy water) any venom oozing from or around the bite.
4. Flush the area copiously with water.
5. Cover it with a clean dressing.
6. Immobilise a bitten limb as for a fracture and transport by stretcher.
7. Get a doctor or send the patient to hospital by ambulance.

In Tropical Climates

Snake bites may be more dangerous, though most are not fatal.

1. Treat as above.
2. Seek medical advice whether anti venom should be given by a doctor. (If the snake has been killed take it with the patient for identification.)
3. Severe pain can be eased by aspirin or paracetemol tablets.
4. If breathing fails give artificial respiration.

Scorpion bites Treat as for snake bites.

THE EFFECTS OF COLD EXPOSURE

Members of outdoor expeditions sometimes show one or more warning signs of approaching collapse from exposure to cold and wet

Slowing down physically and mentally.

Becoming irritable or behaving unreasonably.

Having difficulty in seeing or speaking.

Shivering.

Such a collapse is very dangerous. Act as soon as you suspect it is developing.

immediate treatment

1. Stop and rest. Do not go any further.
2. Prevent further heat loss. Shelter the patient as much as possible. Use blankets or groundsheets as shelter against wind and rain. Pitch a tent over him. Get him into a sleeping bag or wrap bags round him.
3. Give warm sweet drinks such as milk or cocoa.
4. Watch carefully in case emergency resuscitation becomes necessary.
5. Send for a rescue party. The patient must be moved to the base by stretcher. Keep him well covered, particularly over his face and mouth.
6. Get medical help quickly on arrival.

In the home during cold weather, elderly infirm people and babies are at risk. A body temperature below 95°F (35°C) is dangerous and is often unrecognised although the patient is deathly cold to the touch.

Protect the patient against further loss of heat from the body.

1. Allow the body temperature to rise gradually by placing the patient between blankets.
2. Warm the room.
3. Give warm sweet drinks.
4. Do not use hot water bottles or electric blankets.
5. Get medical help.

frost bite

This affects chiefly the fingertips, toes, ear, nose and chin.

1. Remove anything tight near the frost bitten part (glove, ring, garter, boot).
2. Put the affected part under dry warm cover. For example, wrap frost bitten feet up in a blanket or sleeping bag; tuck a frost bitten hand under clothing in the armpit; cover the chin and nose with dry gloved hand.
3. Seek medical help quickly.

DO NOT HEAT BY A FIRE OR A HOT WATER BOTTLE. DO NOT RUB THE SKIN.

THE EFFECTS OF HEAT

Evaporation of perspiration from the skin helps the body to lose excess heat. Wearing loosely fitting clothes in hot weather allows free evaporation with control of the body's temperature.

heat exhaustion

Heat exhaustion is due to abnormal loss of salt and water from the body in very hot circumstances.
Salt is lost in the sweat or with vomiting or diarrhoea.

The patient gradually becomes physically and mentally exhausted. He may have cramps.
He is pale; his skin is moist.
His pulse is fast and weak.
His temperature is normal or a little raised.

treatment

Put the patient in cool surroundings. Get him to drink a mixture of half a **teaspoonful** of salt to one pint (two tumblers) of water.
Get medical aid.

heat stroke

Heat stroke is due to the body not being able to lose excess heat. This dangerous condition occurs mainly in tropical climates where the air has a very high temperature and sometimes may be very humid, without wind.
The patient rapidly becomes restless (and may even become unconscious).
His skin is flushed, dry and burning.
His pulse is fast and strong.
His temperature is extremely high.

treatment

Put the patient in the coolest possible place.
Remove his clothing. Sponge his body repeatedly with cold or tepid water. Fan him (by hand or with an electric fan).
Get medical aid urgently.

prickly heat

An irritating skin condition in the tropics resulting from persistent sweating.

1. Avoid excessive exertion and long hot drinks.

2. Keep the skin well ventilated and as dry as possible with loose-fitting cellular clothing.

3. Cold or tepid showers without soap are advisable, followed by careful drying. A dusting powder is helpful. Dabbing with calamine lotion relieves the irritation.

ACTION IN AN EMERGENCY

what to do

1. Make sure the patient is breathing properly.
   Quickly remove any obstruction in the mouth.
   If necessary give emergency resuscitation (see pages 10 and 90).

2. Stop bleeding (see page 18).

3. Ensure safety from fire, water, traffic, etc.
   If necessary have the traffic stopped.

4. Do not move patient (unless in imminent danger) until
   you know what is wrong and that it is safe to do so.

5. Carefully examine patient and give further treatment if necessary.

6. Place an unconscious patient carefully on his side.
   in the recovery position (see page 49).

7. Uncover the patient as little as possible.

8. Take anti-shock measures (see page 27).

9. Keep crowds well back. Bystanders will be willing to help.
   Choose a reliable one and give him clear instructions.

10. Send for ambulance or doctor, giving details accurately (see page 66).

how to do it

1. Be cool-headed.
2. Take charge calmly and decide the order of your actions.
3. Do not attempt too much.
4. Handle the patient gently.
5. Reassure the patient as much as you can not only by your words but also by showing a smooth quiet efficiency.

sending messages

IF MEDICAL HELP IS NEEDED THE MESSAGE MUST BE CLEAR AND ACCURATE.

1. Decide whether to call a doctor or an ambulance. As a rule:
   Doctor—for simpler home accidents and where an ambulance has to come from far away.
   Ambulance—for serious outdoor accidents
         for asphyxiation
         for severe bleeding
         for severe wounds or burns
         for suspected fractures   Expert advice is needed before moving a patient with a suspected fractured spine
         for patients developing shock
         for unconsciousness.
2. If possible remain with the patient and send the message through a reliable bystander.
3. Write the message down so that no important points are overlooked. Ask that anyone receiving the message by telephone should repeat it to make sure that it has been understood.
4. The message should be brief but complete, giving the following facts:
       The number of patients.
       The nature of the condition and how caused.
       The exact address and, if neccessary, directions on how to get there.
       A request to the doctor for advice on any special action to be taken while waiting if his arrival may be delayed.

after immediate treatment

1. Take the name and address of the patient and of his nearest relative or friend.
2. If the patient is going to hospital, make sure that the relative or friend is told. This can be done through the police.
3. Look after any personal property of the patient or see that it accompanies him to hospital.

TRANSPORT OF PATIENTS

DO NOT TRY TO PRACTISE WITH ANYONE HEAVIER THAN YOURSELF.

walking with support

This is used when the patient is only slightly injured and able to stand.

one first-aider only

1. Stand by the patient's injured side (except when the injury is to the arm, hand or shoulder).

2. Put your arm round his waist and grasp the clothing at the hip.

3. Place his arm round your neck and hold his hand.
   He may get further help from using a walking stick if his other arm and hand are uninjured.

two first-aiders

cradle

This can be used for children or light-weight patients.
Pass one of your arms well beneath his two knees.
Pass the other arm round his back.

pick-a-back

The patient must be conscious and able to hold on.

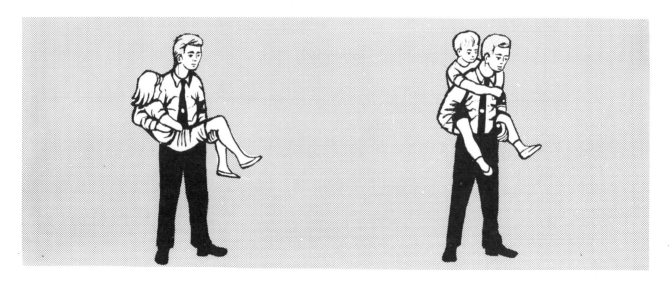

DO NOT TRY TO MOVE A SERIOUSLY ILL PATIENT BY YOURSELF IF HELP IS AVAILABLE.

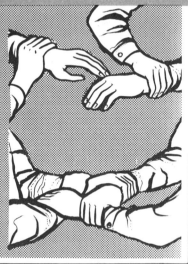

the 4-handed seat

This method is used to carry a patient who is able to use one or both arms.

1. Grasp the left wrist with the right hand.
2. With each free hand grasp the partner's wrist.
3. Tell the patient to place an arm round the neck of each and to sit on the hand seat.
4. Raise up gently and set off together as shown, the right bearer with the right foot and the left bearer with the left foot.

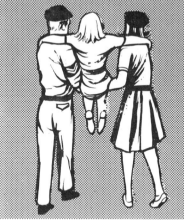

the 2-handed seat

This method is used to carry a helpless patient.

1. Stoop and face each other at each side of the patient.
2. Pass your arm round the patient's back below the shoulders and grip the clothing.
3. Raise the patient's back gently.
4. Pass your other arm under the patient's thighs and clasp your hands in the 'hook grip' shown

here. A folded handkerchief prevents the bearers from hurting each others hands with the finger-nails.
5. Gently raise the patient and set off together as instructed above.

69

kitchen chair support

To move a conscious patient who is not severely injured, on stairs or along passages.

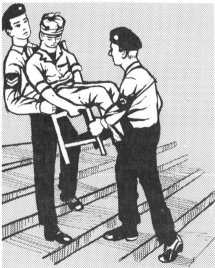

1. Clear the way of obstructions such as furniture.
2. Sit the patient on the chair.
3. One first-aider, behind the chair supports its back and the patient.
4. The other, facing the patient, holds the chair by its front legs.
5. The chair is tilted **slightly** back and lifted, and carried this way.

blanketing a stretcher with only one blanket

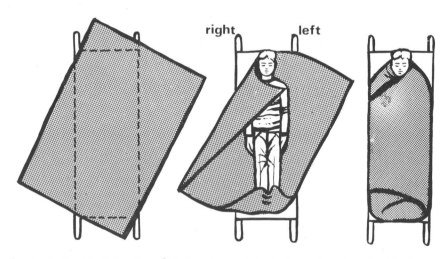

1. Place the blanket diagonally over the stretcher.
2. Place the patient on the stretcher.
3. Bring the point at the head round the patient's neck and over his chest.
4. Bring the point at the foot over the patient's feet. Tuck a small fold between the ankles to prevent these rubbing.
5. Bring the blanket over the patient and tuck in, first the right side of the blanket and then the left side.

with two blankets available

1. Put the **first** blanket lengthwise across the stretcher
   —slightly more to the left edge
   —with the upper edge half covering the handles.

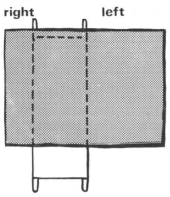

right   left

2. Fold the **second** blanket in three lengthwise.
3. Place it on the stretcher with its upper edge about fifteen inches below the upper edge of the first blanket.
4. Open out folds for the legs and feet.

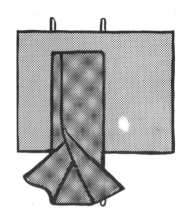

5. Place the patient on the stretcher.
6. Bring the foot of the second blanket up over his feet.
7. Tuck a small fold of this blanket between the ankles to prevent their rubbing.

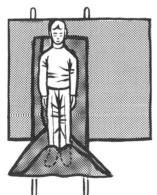

8. Bring over and tuck in the right and then the left open fold of the second blanket.
9. Turn in the upper corners of the first blanket. Bring over and tuck in round the patient the right (shorter) side and then the left (longer) side of this blanket.

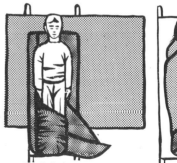
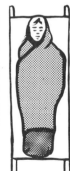

with three blankets available

Between steps 8 and 9 above, double the third blanket lengthwise; lay it over the patient and tuck it in.

loading a stretcher

At least four first-aiders and sometimes six may be needed.

when no blanket is available

1.

Four bearers kneel on their left knees.

The **first** is by the patient's right hip, passing his hands underneath it.

The others are lined up on the patient's left.

The **second** supports the lower limbs.

The **third** supports the patient's hips with his left hand. His right hand holds the right hand of the first bearer using the hook grip described on page 69.

The **fourth** supports the patient's head and shoulders with his right hand. His left hand uses the hook grip to hold the left hand of the first bearer.

2.

At an order from the first bearer the patient is slowly and gently raised and placed on the knees of the other three.

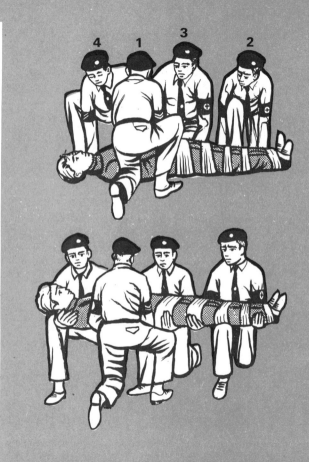

3.

The first bearer now releases his grip and places the stretcher under the patient, making sure that the pillow is in a correct position to receive the head.

4.

The first bearer resumes his position and his grip. At his order the patient is slightly raised from the knees of the others and then carefully and gently lowered on to the stretcher. He is then covered with coats or blankets.

if a blanket is available

Use the method described on page 39.

The position of pillow is not shown.

carrying a stretcher

A stretcher should normally be carried with the patient **feet first.** There are occasions, however, when it is advisable to carry the stretcher with the patient's head first. These are as follows;

If you are going UPhill or UPstairs and the patient's legs are NOT injured.

If you are going DOWNhill or DOWNstairs and the patient's legs ARE injured.

If you are loading an ambulance.

If you are bringing the patient alongside a bed.

over uneven ground

When a stretcher is being carried over uneven ground the four bearers independently adjust the height of the stretcher to keep the patient as level as possible. Over very uneven ground and for short distances they should face inwards.

crossing a wall

1. Rest the front end of the stretcher on the wall while the bearers at the rear keep the stretcher level.
2. The front bearers cross the wall.
3. All the bearers lift and move the stretcher until the rear end rests on the wall.
4. The front bearers hold the stretcher level.
5. The rear bearers cross the wall.

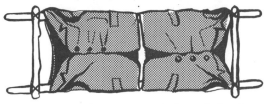

Two strong poles are passed through the sleeves, turned inside out, of two or three coats which are buttoned up.

Holes are made at the bottom corners of one or two strong sacks and the poles are passed through them.

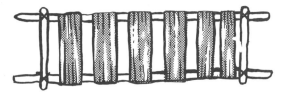

Broad bandages are tied at intervals to two poles. **The poles are kept apart by strips of wood lashed to them at both ends.**

ALWAYS TEST AN IMPROVISED STRETCHER BEFORE USE

A rug, tarpaulin or strong blanket is spread out.
Two stout poles are rolled up in the sides.
Two bearers stand on each side. Each grasps the middle of the covered pole with one hand and near the end with the other.
A door, a hurdle or a wooden gate can be used instead.

The bearers walk sideways, using a cross step.

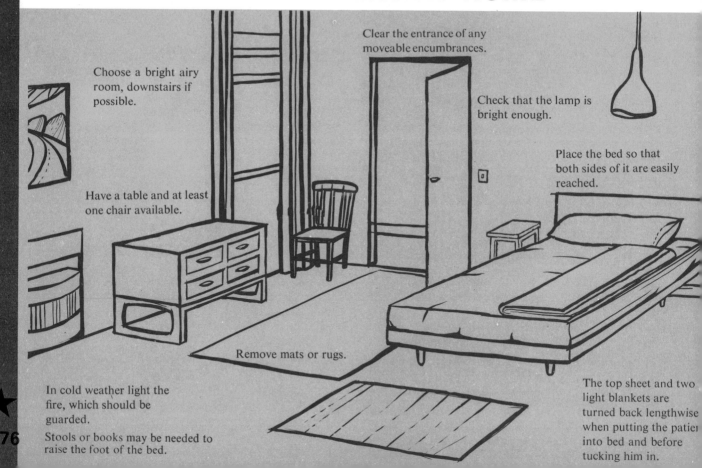

Choose a bright airy room, downstairs if possible.

Clear the entrance of any moveable encumbrances.

Check that the lamp is bright enough.

Place the bed so that both sides of it are easily reached.

Have a table and at least one chair available.

Remove mats or rugs.

In cold weather light the fire, which should be guarded.

Stools or books may be needed to raise the foot of the bed.

The top sheet and two light blankets are turned back lengthwise when putting the patient into bed and before tucking him in.

76

Cover the bed with an old sheet or with newspaper until the patient's soiled clothing is removed.
Where fractures of back, pelvis or lower limbs are suspected, the mattress should be stiffened. Do this by placing boards (or other firm, flat objects like trays) underneath it.
Tuck in the bedclothes loosely for comfort.

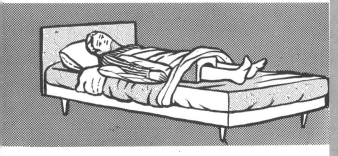

arm injury

Support the arm on a cushion.

leg injury

Improvise a cradle to take the weight of the bedclothes. A deep cardboard box can be used and bedclothes replaced.

1. Have ready washing facilities with soap, nailbrush and clean towel.

2. Cover part of the table surface with a clean towel for the doctor's instruments and dressings.

3. Wash one or two small bowls or basins, rinse with boiling water and cover with clean towels.

4. Place a tumbler of cold water in a convenient position to receive the doctor's thermometer.

5. Have ready a kettle or covered pot containing boiled water which has been allowed to cool.

6. Put out a clean bucket for dirty dressings (which should be burnt later).

7. Have paper and pencil for taking notes.

applying a roller bandage

1. Face the patient.
2. Have the injured part comfortably supported.
3. Bandage from below the injury upwards. Have the beginning of the bandage pointing obliquely a little upwards; fix it by taking a firm turn round the part.
4. Now with a firm and even pressure, bandage from within outwards over the front of the part, with each turn covering two-thirds of the previous one.
5. Finish above the injury, fastening the end with a safety pin or some other suitable method.

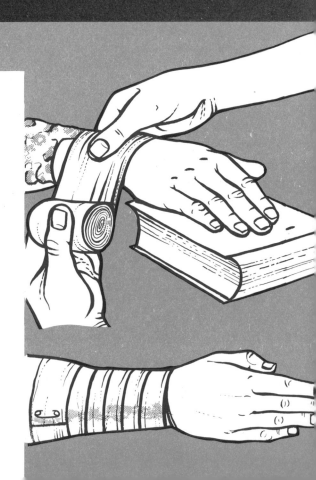

bandage widths for different parts

Finger	1 in.
Head	2 in.
Arm	2–2½ in.
Leg	3 in.
Chest or abdomen	4–6 in.

prepared sterile dressing

This is a combined roller bandage and dressing sterilised and wrapped in a protective covering which is removed only just before use.
The dressing, attached near one end of the bandage, should not be touched by the first-aider who handles only the bandage.

reef knot

A bandage should be tied in a **reef knot** which does not slip, is flat and neat and is easy to untie.
Remember when tying, put
1. left over right and
2. right over left.

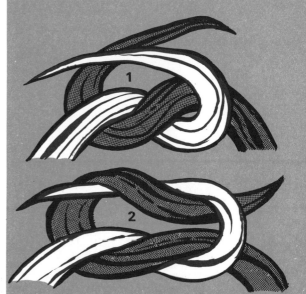

Tuck in ends of bandages to avoid their catching.

the triangular bandage

The triangular bandage is a most useful bandage for first aid because it is easily made or improvised.

It can be made by cutting diagonally into two, a piece of material not less than 36 in. square; this is usually of bleached calico, but any plain material is suitable.

When not in use bandages should be washed and ironed and then stored folded.

packing the triangular bandage

This should be made into a narrow bandage, the two ends brought to meet in the centre, then folded in again and the bandage doubled on itself (as shown below).

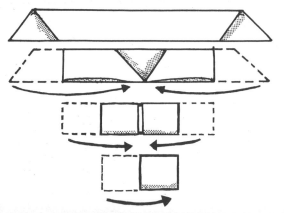

The open bandage is used for the arm sling, the triangular sling and to keep dressings in place.

When the open bandage is used a narrow hem should be turned in along the base.

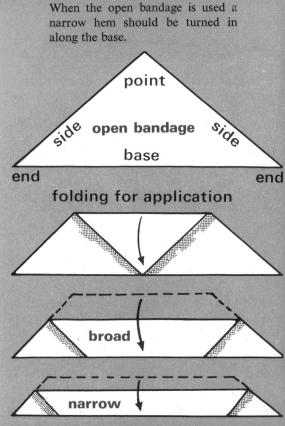

folding for application

The broad or narrow bandages are used for keeping dressings firmly in place, and for immobilising fractur

ring pad

A ring pad is made from a narrow fold bandage.

1. A couple of turns are looped round the fingers.

1.

2.

3.

2. The free end is now wound firmly round the loop until the whole has been covered.

3. The end is now tucked in and a firm ring has been formed.

The ring pad is used to give encircling pressure and protection where direct pressure on the wound would be wrong — for instance, a fracture at the wrist or a foreign body like a piece of glass embedded in the wound.

If possible a clean dressing should be placed over the wound before the ring pad is put on.

the arm sling

This is used for injuries to ribs, upper arm and forearm.

1. Support the forearm and place the bandage over the front of the body bringing the upper end round the neck and well over the injured shoulder.

2. Move the injured arm on to the bandage with the hand slightly higher than the elbow.

3. Bring the lower end up over the forearm and tie a reef knot in front of the shoulder of the injured side.

4. Turn the corner at the elbow forward, and pin it.

5. Fold in the edges if too large.

6. Leave the fingertips exposed so that the circulation may be tested.

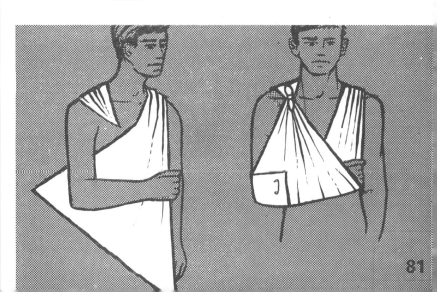

triangular sling

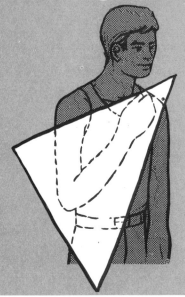  

This is used for injuries to collar bone and hand.

1. Place the patient's forearm across his chest so that his fingers point towards the uninjured shoulder, and the palm of the hand rests on the chest.

2. Lay an open bandage over the fore-arm with one end over the hand, and the point well beyond the elbow.

3. Steady the limb and tuck the base of the bandage well under the hand, forearm and elbow.

4. Bring the lower end under the bent elbow and up round the back to the uninjured shoulder.

5. Tie both ends together in the hollow above the collar bone.

6. Tuck the point in between the fore-arm and the bandage in front, making a fold.

7. Turn this fold backwards over the lower part of the arm and pin it.

When applying a sling, it is important to support the injured arm carefully until the sling is secured and takes the weight of the arm.

improvised slings

Improvised slings can be made in the following ways:

Place the injured arm inside the buttoned-up coat or waistcoat. Pin the sleeve to the lapel of the coat if necessary.

Turn up the bottom edge of the coat and pin it to the opposite lapel.

Use belts, braces, neck-ties or tapes.

scalp bandage

1. Place the base over the forehead just above the eyebrows.
2. Cross the ends over the point behind the head and carry forward to the forehead.
3. Tie the knot in the centre of the forehead.
4. Pull the point down, then turn it up and pin.

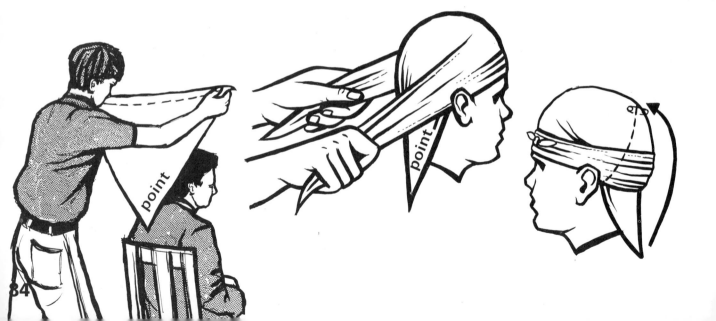

hand or foot bandage

1. Place the hand (or foot) on a fully open bandage with the point away from the patient. Fold the point over the hand (or instep).

2. Bring the ends over and round the wrist (or ankle).

3. Cross them and tie over the point.

4. Bring the point down over the knot and pin it.

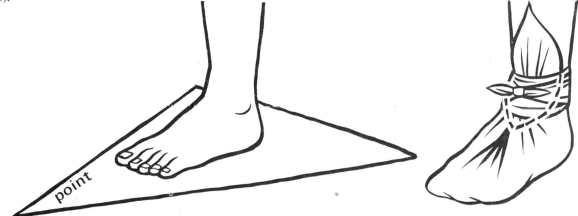

elbow or knee bandage

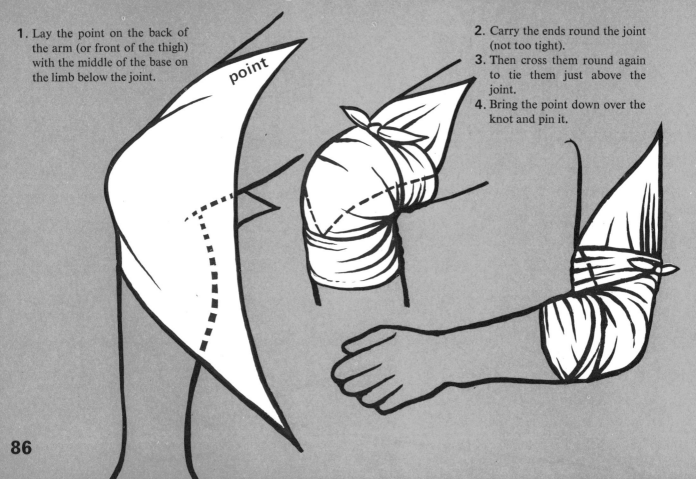

1. Lay the point on the back of the arm (or front of the thigh) with the middle of the base on the limb below the joint.

point

2. Carry the ends round the joint (not too tight).
3. Then cross them round again to tie them just above the joint.
4. Bring the point down over the knot and pin it.

hip bandage

(2 bandages required)

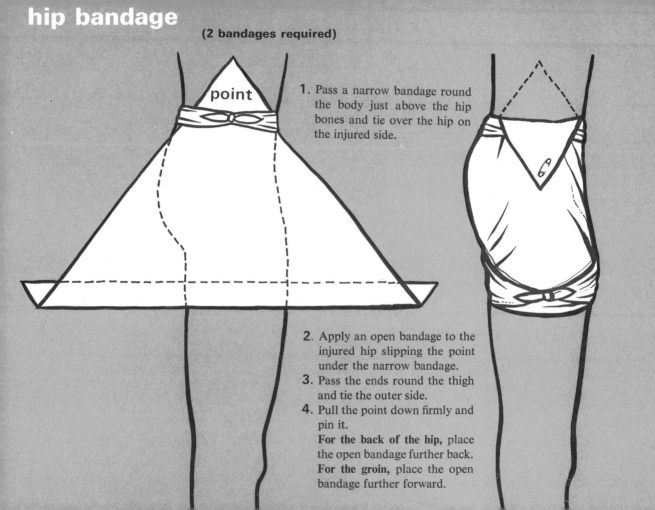

point

1. Pass a narrow bandage round the body just above the hip bones and tie over the hip on the injured side.

2. Apply an open bandage to the injured hip slipping the point under the narrow bandage.
3. Pass the ends round the thigh and tie the outer side.
4. Pull the point down firmly and pin it.
   For the back of the hip, place the open bandage further back.
   For the groin, place the open bandage further forward.

shoulder bandage (2 bandages required)

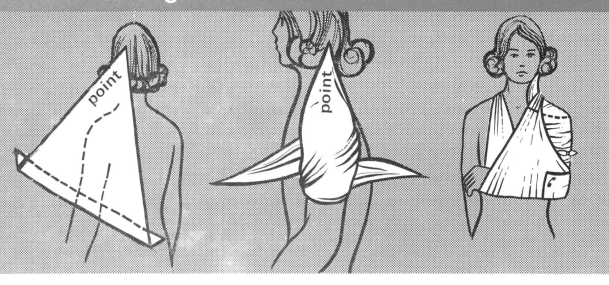

1. Apply an open bandage with its centre over the injured shoulder.

2. Pass the ends round the middle of the upper arm and tie off on the outer side.

3. Apply an arm sling. Turn the point down over the knot and pin it.

1. Place the point over the shoulder.

2. Pass the ends backwards round the body and tie in a reef knot directly below the point, leaving one end long.

3. Tie this long end of the knot to the point.

Apply the bandage to the patient's back and proceed as before.

APPENDIX

If after you have given artificial respiration for four breaths with successful movement of the patient's chest:

1. His colour remains a deathly blue-grey (especially the lips, nails, tip of the nose and under the eyelids).
2. The pupils of his eyes (central dark circles) are widely dilated.
3. No carotid pulse can be felt at the side of the neck (see page 16).

THIS MEANS THE HEART HAS STOPPED. IMMEDIATELY TRY TO REVIVE ITS BEAT.

1. Have the patient on his back on a firm surface (preferably the floor).
2. Slap the chest smartly over the lower part of the breast bone. This may start the beat. If it does not:
3. Kneel by the patient. Put the 'heel' of one hand on the lower end of the breast bone; cover it with the heel of your other hand (but keep your palms and fingers off the chest.)
4. Press the lower end of the breast bone down firmly but evenly by rocking forward on your straight arms. Do this

> **for adults** once a second,
>
> **for children** a little faster—about 80 times a minute. Less force is needed; the pressure of the heel of one hand is enough.
>
> **for babies** a hundred times a minute, using the pressure of two fingers only.

The breast bone pressed repeatedly down against the heart makes the blood circulate (and may start the heart beating on its own again).

> SUCCESS IS JUDGED BY:
> 1. The patient's colour improving.
> 2. The pupils of his eyes contracting to their normal size.
> 3. Return of the carotid pulse (see page 16). This, however, is not always easily felt.

90

Get your position accurately by knowing the landmarks of the chest. Compression badly applied may injure ribs or other structures. With care this risk may be minimised by:

1. Using only the heel of the hands (or the fingers in the case of babies).
2. Pressing only on the lower half of the breast bone.
3. Avoiding jerky action.

A second is longer than you think. Practise with a watch by your side.

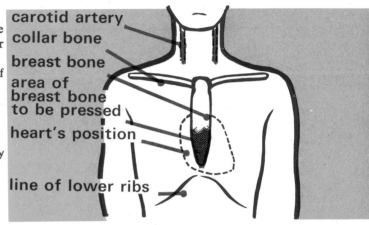

carotid artery
collar bone
breast bone
area of breast bone to be pressed
heart's position
line of lower ribs

NEVER GIVE HEART COMPRESSION IF THE HEART IS BEATING SPONTANEOUSLY

The method and use of heart compression is to be taught by a doctor

When the heart has stopped, so has breathing. Whenever heart compression is needed so is artificial respiration.

If you are alone: alternate artificial respiration with heart compression, moving smoothly and quickly from one to the other 2 quick inflations of the lungs are followed by 15 heart compressions.
If you have help: one first aider does mouth-to-mouth breathing, the other attends to heart compression. They do not act together but alternate one inflation with 5 heart compressions.

Syllabus-
Junior First Aid Certificate

Session 1
Scope of First Aid.
Breathing. Asphyxia.
Artificial Respiration. Mouth-to-Mouth (to-nose) resuscitation (using manikin) including after care (placing patient in recovery position).
Electric Shock — dangers involved,

Session 2
Shock and its prevention.
Circulation of the Blood. The pulse.
Bleeding and Wounds. External bleeding. Control of bleeding by finger pressure, pad and bandage. Bandage for cut in the palm of the hand. Triangular sling and reef knot. Use of roller bandages.

Session 3
Bleeding and Wounds (*continued*). Bleeding from the nose, ear, and tooth socket and their management. Wounds and grazes. Dressing of wounds including use of prepared sterile dressings and emergency dressings. Bruises, including making a cold compress. Splinters. Arm sling. Ring pad.

Session 4
The Skeleton.
Fractures — General. Management of fractures of ribs, collar bone and upper limb including hand.

Session 5
Fractures (*continued*). Management of fractures of the lower limb including foot. Danger of moving fractured spine.

Session 6
Joints — injuries to joints (sprains, dislocations, displaced cartilage of the knee) and their management.
Muscles — injuries to muscles (strains) and their management.

Session 7
The Nervous System. Unconsciousness. Examination and care of the unconscious patient. Use of recovery position. Fainting and its management. Convulsions in young children.

Session 8
Burns and Scalds. Management of burns and scalds. Clothes catching fire. Sunburn.

Session 9
Poisoning and its management.
Miscellaneous conditions including cramp, winding and foreign bodies in the eye, nose and throat. Insect stings. Blisters caused by rubbing.

Session 10
Action in an Emergency.
Sending messages — practice in writing messages.
Transport of Patients — walking with support; use of hand seats; kitchen chair method.

Session 11
Revision.

Practice in bandaging should be incorporated throughout.

Procedures on pages marked by a broad red edge and a black star are to be omitted.

Syllabus—
Junior First Aid Proficiency

ocedures marked by a broad red edge and a black star are included.

Session 1
Artificial Respiration. Revision of asphyxia and mouth-to-mouth (to-nose) resuscitation. Holger Nielsen method.

Session 2
Circulatory System and Shock. Revision of control of external bleeding and dressing of wounds. Management of bleeding from varicose veins. Internal bleeding.

Session 3
Injuries to Bones, Joints and Muscles. Revision of skeleton, and management of simple fractures, sprains, dislocations and strains. Management of fractures of jaw and pelvis. Management of complicated fracture of the ribs.

Session 4
Fractures (*continued*). Revision of other fractures. Management of fractures of lower limb for a difficult journey, and of fractured spine.
Revision of management of Burns and Scalds.

Session 5
The Nervous System. Revision of nervous system and unconsciousness. Brain injuries and their management. Hysteria, epilepsy and their management.
Revision of management of Poisoning.

Session 6
Miscellaneous Conditions. Revision of miscellaneous conditions.
Treatment of snake bite.
Effects of heat and cold.
Revision of transport of patients. Blanketing, loading and carrying of stretchers. Improvised stretchers.
Preparing for a patient at home.

Session 7
Action in an Emergency. Staging of a typical incident with simulated casualties.
Revision.

Practice in bandaging should be incorporated throughout.

FURTHER NOTES FOR USE IN HOT CLIMATES

Acute Diarrhoea and Vomiting

Where this has been persistent, the body has lost both fluids and also important salts. This can quickly have a seriously weakening effect, especially in young children who will need rapid admission to hospital.

Adults will require sweetened fluids and also water to which common salt has been added. (Half teaspoonful to the pint.)

In all cases seek medical advice.

Dog Bites

Wherever there is a risk of rabies:

1. The patient (after the usual treatment of the wound) should be referred to a doctor for a decision about rabic treatment.

2. The dog should, if possible, be chained up in isolation for 14 days' observation to see whether he develops signs of rabies.

Leech and Tick Bites

1. Do not try to pull the creature off.
   Apply common salt or the glowing end of a cigarette to it to make it drop off.

2. Clean the area with soap and water.

3. Relieve itching with anti-histamine cream if available.

4. Cover with a dry dressing.

INDEX

KNOW THE GAME ?

There are now over 80 books in this well-known series. They are fully illustrated and give clear, concise explanations of the rules and basic principles of every popular sport and pastime. Each book is prepared with the official Association and the whole series is always kept up-to-date

THERE IS A "KNOW THE GAME" BOOK ON YOUR SPORT

ANGLING . AIR TRAVEL . ARCHERY . ASSOCIATION FOOTBALL . ATHLETICS . BATINTON . BADMINTON BALLROOM DANCING . BASKETBALL . BILLIARDS AND SNOOKER . BOATING . BOWLS . CONTRACT BRIDGE . CARAVANNING . CAMPING . CHESS CRICKET . CROQUET . CYCLING . FENCING . GOLF GYMNASTICS . ICE AND ROLLER SKATING . INN GAMES . JUDO . KEEPING FIT FOR ALL AGES LACROSSE . LATIN AMERICAN DANCING . LAWN TENNIS . LIFE SAVING . MOTOR BOATING AND WATER SKI-ING . MAP READING . MEN'S HOCKEY PHOTOGRAPHY   LEARNING TO FLY

MODEL MAKING . MOTOR CYCLING . MOTOR SPORT NETBALL . OLD TIME DANCING . ORIENTEERING   . PIGEON RACING . POTHOLING . RACING . RAMBLING AND YOUTH HOSTELLING . ROCK CLIMBING ROUNDERS . RUGBY LEAGUE FOOTBALL . RUGBY UNION FOOTBALL . SAILING . SCHOOLBOY BOXING SHOT GUN SHOOTING . SHOW JUMPING . SKI-ING SQUASH RACKETS   .   STAMP COLLECTING SWIMMING . SWIMMING TO WIN . TABLE TENNIS TEN PIN BOWLING . TRAMPOLINING . UNDERWATER SWIMMING . VOLLEYBALL . WOMEN'S HOCKEY WRESTLING

Fully illustrated   .   Size $5\frac{1}{4}$ ins. x 8 ins. .   Price $17\frac{1}{2}$p to 25p

available from your sports dealer or bookshop
or from E.P. Publishing Limited, East Ardsley, Wakefield, Yorkshire.

A.B.C. OF NURSING

Contains detailed information on the essentials of nursing, compiled in a handy reference form in alphabetical order.

52 pages. Over 50 illustrations   *Size 8″ x 5″*   Price 17½p net.

A.B.C. OF FIRST AID

A companion volume to the above with instructions for First Aid treatment produced for the British Red Cross Society.

36 pages. 40 illustrations   *Size 8″ x 5″*   Price 17½p net.

A.B.C. OF CHILD CARE

This book has been produced for the British Red Cross Society. This book presents in alphabetical order information about the more common illnesses and accidents to which young children are exposed and gives information about how these can be prevented and treated.

56 pages. Fully illustrated   *Size 8″ x 5″*   Price 17½p net.

FIRST AID JUNIOR MANUAL

This will replace the previous Junior First Aid Manual. The book is completely rewritten and contains many more pages incorporating much new material.

96 pages. Fully illustrated   *Size 5″ x 8″*   Price 25p net.

JUNIOR MOTHERCRAFT MANUAL

An invaluable textbook for hygiene lessons for older girls in schools, illustrating the practical side of the care of young babies and children. It covers the various stages of development from infancy to the age of five years, and describes the nursery, layette, care and daily routine of the baby and his mental and physical development. Published for the British Red Cross Society.

64 pages. Fully illustrated   *Size 5″ x 8″*   Price 17½p net.

JUNIOR NURSING MANUAL

Contains fully illustrated guidance on the nursing care of the sick; it also covers topics ranging from choice of a sick room to suitable diets, medicines and infectious diseases. Useful in girls' schools, particularly where a Nursing or Pre-Nursing Course is organised.

68 pages. Fully illustrated   *Size 5″ x 8″*   Price 17½p net.

JUNIOR HEALTH AND HYGIENE MANUAL

Deals with personal hygiene and explains how and why cleanliness and personal care are necessary. Further chapters describe how the home should be kept clean, how the town services work and how important fresh air and water are. An explanation is given of the spread of disease and the precautions that can be taken to prevent this.
A British Red Cross Society book.

64 pages. Fully illustrated   *Size 5″ x 8″*   Price 17½p net.

Published jointly by

THE BRITISH RED CROSS SOCIETY   *and*   **EP PUBLISHING LIMITED**

9 Grosvenor Crescent
London SW1 7EJ

East Ardsley,
Wakefield, Yorkshire.